Gastric Bypass Cookbook:

Overcome Your Food Addiction & Heavy Fast to the Ashes through a Meal Plan with Tested, Tasty, & Balanced Recipes | Phoenix Bariatric Diet Method

Copyright © 2022

Sarah Roslin

TABLE OF CONTENTS

1   THE BASICS OF BARIATRIC SURGERY

What is Bariatric Surgery

One of the four weight-loss procedures that are legal in the United States is referred to as "Bariatric Surgery." It can be classified as one of four main operations: the Roux-en-Y gastric bypass, the more popular gastric band surgery, the intricate biliopancreatic diversion with a duodenal switch, and the vertical sleeve gastrectomy, which forms the basis of this book. The second surgery reduces your stomach's ability to store food by removing a significant portion of it. Since you are forced to eat smaller portions as a result of having this surgery, reading this book will help you on your quest to losing weight. The mainstay of most dietary plans is little, frequent meals since your stomach will stay fuller longer if it digests smaller, more regular meals opposed than gorging on a big meal all at once.

1.1   What is the type of bariatric surgery and the differences?

Bariatric surgery types

There are benefits and drawbacks to each form of bariatric surgery. Talk about them with your doctor, of course. Examples of typical bariatric surgery techniques are provided below:

Roux-en-Y Gastric bypass. This procedure for gastric bypass is the most widely used one. Typically, this process cannot be undone. It works by reducing nutrient absorption and restricting how much food you can eat at once.

To divide the top of the stomach from the rest of the stomach, the surgeon makes a cut. The resulting pouch, which is about the size of a walnut, might only carry a little over an ounce of food. The stomach can typically accommodate three pints of food..

The surgeon will next partially cut and suture the small intestine onto the pouch. Following the entry into this little stomach pouch, food immediately makes its way to the that is attached to it, the small intestine. Food moves straight from the mouth to the small intestine, skipping the majority of the stomach and the first part of the small intestine.

Gastric sleeve surgery. By removing around 80% of the stomach during a sleeve gastrectomy, a long, tube-like pouch is left behind. There is less room for food in this smaller stomach. Additionally, it creates less ghrelin, a hormone that controls hunger, which may reduce the desire to eat.

This treatment has benefits including considerable weight loss and no gut rerouting. Additionally, compared to most other procedures, a sleeve gastrectomy requires a shorter hospital stay.

Duodenal switch with biliopancreatic diversion. In the first stage of this two-part treatment, a sleeve gastrectomy-like technique is carried out. Bypassing the majority of the intestine, the second procedure (duodenal switch and biliopancreatic diversion) connects the terminal a section of the intestine's duodenal connection, which is located close to the stomach.

This procedure both restricts how much you can consume and decreases nutrient absorption. Although it is quite successful, there are higher risks associated with it, such as starvation and vitamin deficiencies.

The weight-loss procedure that is best for you will depend on your particular circumstances. Your body mass index, dietary habits, other medical conditions, previous surgeries, and the dangers of each procedure are just a few of the variables your surgeon will consider.

1.2 What's the difference between these two surgeries?

The main difference between these two treatments is that the gastric sleeve is only restrictive. Contrarily, gastric bypass is both limiting and malabsorptive..

Your food portions will be smaller after a gastric bypass, and your body will take in fewer calories. You must choose wisely when it comes to your diet if you want to keep your body in good shape. Most people who have gastric bypass require lifelong dietary supplements. This guarantees that you receive the proper dosage of essential nutrients, including vitamins and minerals.

Otherwise, there are many similarities between gastric sleeve and gastric bypass. By limiting your intake of food, both operations assist you in losing excess weight.

1.3 Requirements to qualify for gastric sleeve and gastric bypass surgery

Gastric Sleeve Surgery

Up to 70% of your stomach may be surgically removed during sleeve gastrectomy, often known as gastric sleeve surgery.

What good does that do you, though?

Since a huge portion of your stomach has been eliminated, the goal is to make you feel satisfied after consuming significantly less food than previously. As a smaller stomach will produce less ghrelin, the hormone that causes hunger, you will also feel less hungry as a result of this.

People who are obese and experiencing medical disorders brought on by their weight are advised to have an operation.

Generally speaking, a patient's body mass index determines whether they can have weight-loss surgery (BMI). Typically, adults with a BMI of 40 or more are taken into account, as well as adolescents with a BMI of 35 and an obesity-related illness.

Adults who fit the following criteria may be qualified for the gastric sleeve **Procedure:**

- 40 or greater BMI
- Being obese with a BMI of 35 or above and having at least one illness
- Have a condition that is exacerbated by fat, such as diabetes, back discomfort, sleep apnea, joint difficulties, or another problem
- At least six months' worth of unsuccessful attempts to lose weight using different methods

If an adolescent satisfies the requirements listed below, they may be eligible for the gastric sleeve **Procedure:**

- A BMI of 40 or above and any condition linked to obesity
- BMI of 35 or above and a serious condition associated with obesity

If you have a lower BMI yet a serious obesity-related condition, you can be qualified for gastric sleeve surgery.

Gastric Bypass

By altering the digestive tract, bariatric surgery, which includes gastric bypass and other weight loss procedures, aids in weight loss. There are various distinct kinds of bariatric operations, some of which limit the amount of food that the stomach can contain while others lower the number of nutrients that the body can absorb. Some approaches provide both, while others do not.

The recommended course of treatment is not necessarily bariatric surgery, despite the fact that it has been proved to be extremely effective. Keep in mind that bariatric surgery can be a severe procedure with risks and negative effects. As a result, fulfilling certain criteria is necessary to receive authorization for bariatric treatment.

The following conditions must be met before having According to the American Society for Metabolic and Bariatric Surgery, bariatric surgery (AMBS):

- Having a body mass index (BMI) exceeding 40 or being at least 100 pounds overweight. Your BMI may be estimated right here.
- A BMI greater than or equal to one or more obesity-related comorbidities, such as type 2 diabetes, heart disease, stroke, hypertension, or non-alcoholic fatty liver disease.
- Failure for a while to lose weight in a healthy way
- Those who desire to change their lifestyles after having bariatric surgery should consider the operation. A dietitian, an exercise physiologist, and a mental health specialist may be requested to see patients again.

1.4 Risks and Complications of these Surgeries (also after years from the surgery)

The risk of problems and nutritional deficits increases with how comprehensive the bypass operation is. Patients who have had their normal digestive system significantly bypassed need to be closely watched as well as take special diets and drugs for the rest of their lives.

Ten to twenty percent of patients who undergo weight-loss surgery need further procedures to address problems. The most frequent consequences requiring additional surgery are abdominal hernias.

Leakage through staples or sutures, stomach or small intestine ulcers, blood clots in the lungs or legs, straining of the pouch or esophagus, persistent vomiting and abdominal pain, gallbladder inflammation, and inability to lose weight are unusual risks of gastric bypass surgery (very rare).

Gallstones form in more than one-third of obese people who undergo gastric surgery. Gallstones are cholesterol and other material-containing clumps that develop in the gallbladder. A person's chance of acquiring gallstones rises during rapid or significant weight reduction.

By taking extra bile salts for the first six months after surgery, gallstones can be avoided.

Anemia, osteoporosis, and metabolic bone disease are among the nutritional deficits that nearly 30% of individuals who have weight-loss surgery develop. By maintaining vitamin and mineral intake, these deficiencies can be prevented.

Women of childbearing age should postpone getting pregnant for 18 to 2 years, or until their weight stabilizes, as fast weight loss and nutritional deficits can be harmful to an unborn child.

Although gastric bypass surgeries can be undone, patients should carefully weigh all the advantages and disadvantages before deciding to undergo this procedure.

Among the hazards of bariatric surgery are:

- Reflux of acid
- Hazards associated with anesthesia
- Persistent diarrhea and vomiting
- Expanding of the esophagus

- Being unable to consume certain foods
- Infection
- Stomach obstruction Gaining or failing to shed weight

Long-Term Risks of Bariatric Surgery

Long-term hazards associated with bariatric surgery include:

- Ulcers
- Dumping syndrome, a condition that can lead to symptoms like nausea and dizziness
- Bowel obstruction
- Malnutrition
- Low blood sugar
- Hernias
- Vomiting

Overview of the Risks and Complications of Bariatric Surgery, Organized by Organ

By bariatric technique, risks and adverse effects differ. The hazards of gastric bypass and gastric sleeve are briefly discussed in the list below, which is not all-inclusive. Your bariatric surgeon will make sure you are aware of the dangers and potential side effects of your particular treatment.

Gastric bypass dangers

- Syndrome of "Breakage Dumping"(Risk increases with rapid or significant weight loss)
- Gallstones
- Hernia
- Internal bleeding or significant surgical wound hemorrhage
- Leakage
- Intestinal or stomach perforation
- Bowel blockage or pouch/anastomotic obstruction
- Calorie or protein malnutrition
- Heart and/or pulmonary issues
- Skin dissection
- Damage to the spleen or another organ
- Ulcers in the stomach or intestines
- Stricture
- Iron or vitamin deficiency

Gastric Sleeve Risks

- Clots of blood
- (Risk increases with rapid or significant weight loss) Gallstones
- Hernia
- Internal bleeding or significant surgical wound hemorrhage
- Leakage
- intestinal or stomach perforation
- skin dissection
- Stricture
- iron or vitamin deficiency

1.5   Comparison Between the Recovery after the two Surgeries

The method for bariatric surgery is generally safe. According to the American Society for Metabolic and Bariatric Surgery, there is a 4% chance of a major consequence. This is significantly less likely than the chance of serious obesity-related health problems.

- Any surgery, including bariatric surgery, may be complicated by a number of problems, such as:
- losing blood (hemorrhage)

- the emergence of blood clots in your lungs or leg (deep vein thrombosis) (pulmonary embolism)
- general anesthesia side affects incisional infection
- perioperative discomfort pneumonia

Following bariatric surgery, potential side effects include:

- vitamin and nutritional deficits and gallstones
- eating too rapidly, eating sweet, fried, or fatty foods, or consuming dairy might cause nausea, sweating, and extreme diarrhea (dumping syndrome)
- loose or sagging skin

Complications after having a gastric sleeve

Gastric sleeve surgery-specific complications include:

- stomach obstruction caused by stenosis along the stomach pouch and acid reflux leakage of stomach fluid
- problems following gastric bypass surgery

Gastric bypass-specific complications include:

- Heightened sensitivity to alcohol and a greater risk of nutritional deficiencies as a result of skipping some of your small intestines
- peptic ulcers
- digestive blockage
- stomach piercing

1.6 Final comparison of the Pros and cons of the two surgeries

Pros and cons of gastric sleeve surgery

Pros of a gastric sleeve

- Up to 65% of your excess body weight can be lost.
- Because it is a one-step process, the chance of problems is lower.
- When compared to gastric bypass, the recovery is quicker.
- Vitamin and nutrient absorption problems are less common.
- Less often, the dumping syndrome occurs.

Cons of a gastric sleeve

- Compared to gastric bypass, weight loss is less.
- Losing weight takes longer.
- It cannot be undone.
- It could result in acid reflux.

Pros and cons of gastric bypass surgery

Pros of gastric bypass

- Up to 80% of your excess body weight can be lost.
- A bypass of the digestive tract reduces calorie absorption.
- As opposed to gastric sleeve surgery, you lose weight more quickly.
- Although challenging, it is reversible.

Cons of gastric bypass

- Due to the two-step nature of the procedure, problems are more likely.
- Compared to gastric sleeve surgery, the recovery period is lengthier.
- The malabsorption of vitamins and nutrients brought on by intestinal bypass can result in shortages.
- The dumped syndrome is more prevalent.

2   GASTRIC BYPASS SURGERY

2.1 Why do it (benefits of weight loss)

Gastric bypass is a popular method of bariatric surgery. If you have tried and failed to lose weight through diet and exercise, or if your weight is causing serious health problems, you may be a candidate for a gastric bypass treatment. A gastric bypass is a weight-loss surgery that involves removing a small pouch from the stomach and connecting it directly to the small intestine. Following a gastric bypass, food goes via this small pouch in the stomach and into the small intestine, bypassing the remainder of the stomach and the first section of the small intestine.

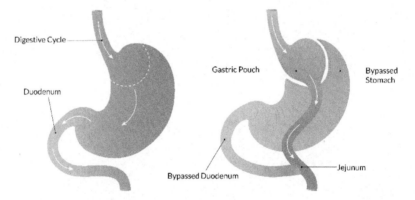

Your stomach gets smaller after gastric bypass surgery, limiting how much you can consume. In order to reduce how much food is absorbed, the surgeon will also reroute or "bypass" a portion of your digestive tract.

The most popular gastric bypass The Roux-en-Y technique is carried out in the United States. Small cuts can be used by surgeons, which has a speedier recovery period than more involved surgery. By stitching a section of the stomach together or by vertical banding, the surgeon first creates a tiny stomach pouch. This restricts how much food you can eat. The surgeon then joins a tiny intestinal segment in a Y form to the pouch. As a result, food bypasses a portion of your digestive tract. You assimilate less calories and nutrients as a result. To assist you in losing additional weight and lower your risk of serious, potentially fatal, weight-related health issues, like:

- Diabetes type 2
- Elevated blood pressure
- Heart condition
- Stroke
- High triglycerides
- Cancer
- The disease of the gastroesophageal reflux
- Obstructive snoring
- Infertility

Gastric bypass is usually only carried out after you've made an effort to reduce weight by altering you're eating and exercise routines.

2.2 What happens during the surgery?

You will be given a general anesthesia before the operation. There will be no pain, and you'll feel tired. A gastric bypass involves two stages:

1. After the first step, your stomach shrinks. Your surgeon uses staples to divide your stomach into a smaller upper portion and a larger lower region. The food you eat will enter the pouch, which is the upper section of your stomach. The sack is walnut in size. Within, just around 1 ounce (oz) or 28 grams (g) of food can fit. As a result, you will eat less and lose weight.
2. The next step is the bypass. Your surgeon connects the jejunum, a short section of your small intestine, to a tiny hole in your pouch. Food can now flow from the pouch into your small intestine thanks to this new aperture. Because of this, you'll be able to cut back on your caloric intake.

There are two ways to do a gastric bypass. With open surgery, your stomach is exposed after a significant surgical incision is made. The stomach, small intestine, and other organs are worked on during the bypass. A laparoscope, a tiny camera used in this surgery, is another option. You carry this camera inside your abdomen. The procedure is known as a laparoscopy. The scope gives the surgeon access to your belly inside. In this operation:

*   Your stomach receives 4 to 6 little cuts from the surgeon.
*   Through these cuts, the surgical scope and other equipment are inserted.
*   The operating room's visual monitor is linked to the camera. This enables the surgeon to see into your tummy while they do the procedure.

Laparoscopy has several benefits over open surgery, including:

*   less time in the hospital and quicker recovery
*   fewer pains
*   less scars and a decreased chance of developing an infection or hernia

In this procedure, 2 to 4 hours are needed.

2.3 FAQ about the recovery phase (what' happen after the surgery including side effects and solutions, etc.)

How much weight are you going to lose?

Find out exactly what to expect by asking your doctor. It might be influenced, in part, by your current weight and the kind of operation you have. A more often performed weight loss procedure is the sleeve gastrectomy. A sleeve gastrectomy results in roughly 40% of the excess weight is lost. Following gastric bypass surgery, people typically lose 60% of the excess weight they had. The gastric band is no longer a widely used weight loss procedure. Many people discover that over the course of months, their weight loss fluctuates, lowering, then leveling off, and then dropping once again. You could continue losing weight for up to 2 or 3 years following surgery, depending on the treatment.

How is the operation performed?

The procedure is carried out through six tiny, half-inch incisions (laparoscopic surgery). Through tubes inside these incisions, known as ports, laparoscopic surgical tools are inserted, including a small camera. Rarely, a laparotomy or "open" gastric bypass may be required.

What makes it a Roux-en-Y?

A: It alludes to the small bowel connection's 'Y' form. The small bowel will now receive food that has been chewed and swallowed after being sliced during the procedure and rejoined at one end of the newly constructed pouch (the new stomach). During the procedure, none of the bowels is removed. An anastomosis is a new link between the small intestine and the stomach pouch. This little aperture, also known as the Roux limb, helps to restrict the movement of food migrating from the pouch into this section of the small bowel (after a French surgeon, Roux). The right arm of the "Y" is the Roux limb. The left arm of the "Y" represents the piece of the bowel that was left outside and is still connected to the stomach. It transports the digestive juices created by the liver, pancreas, and some of the small bowel itself, as well as the acids produced in the stomach residual, including insulin. The "Y's" two arms are once more joined.

Even though I've already had open stomach surgery, can I still have my procedure done laparoscopically?

A: Your surgeon will consider each patient individually. After open abdominal surgery or other laparoscopic abdominal procedures, a laparoscopic gastric bypass is an option. Every patient has the right to be offered the option of choosing minimally invasive surgery, according to our surgeons.

My Body Mass Index is high (BMI). Is laparoscopic gastric bypass still an option?

A patient with a BMI of 88 underwent laparoscopic gastric bypass surgery with great success. Extreme physical requirements and a high BMI can be too much of a problem for a different surgical team with less training. We don't rule someone out for laparoscopic surgery based only on their BMI. You will be assessed by your surgeon on an individual basis. One of the most skilled and well-known teams of bariatric and minimally invasive surgeons in the Midwest may be found at NorthShore University Health System. Once more, our doctors are of the opinion that every patient has the right to be offered the option of electing minimally invasive surgery.

What Kind of Recovery Can We Expect?

The majority of gastric bypass operations are laparoscopic, which means the doctor makes tiny incisions. The recuperation period is shortened as a result. Most patients spend 2 to 3 days in the hospital and return to their regular activities in 3 to 5 weeks. Healing takes longer if the procedure must be "open," which requires the surgeon to make a wider incision.

What Consequences Might There Be?

Surgery for weight loss may result in both short- and long-term consequences. Depending on the procedure, different long-term dangers exist. A problem of some kind affects about 40% of people. There are only about 5% significant problems. Visit your doctor if you do experience any issues that worry you. Several frequent adverse effects include:

- Following weight loss surgery, constipation is typical. You can get advice from your doctor on how to address it. Avoid granular fiber, such as psyllium or Metamucil, as these may cause blockages.
- Dumping syndrome happens after consuming meals heavy in sugar following weight loss surgery. Sodas or fruit juices are commonly to blame. You can feel weak and queasy from the fast-moving sugary meal.
- Gallstones can develop often after rapid weight loss. Following gastric bypass surgery, gallstones can develop in up to 50% of patients, however, they normally don't cause any harm. Gallstones can occasionally result in nausea, vomiting, and abdominal pain. 15% to 25% of people who undergo gastric bypass surgery also need to have their gallbladders removed.

- Wound infections might appear up to three weeks after surgery. Examples of symptoms include redness, warmth, discomfort, or thick discharge (pus) from the surgical site. For wound infections, antibiotics are required, and more surgery may be required.
- Bloody or reddish stools, often known as bowel bleeding, can be quite harmful. Visit an emergency room if necessary, or immediately let your doctor know.
- Less than 1% of the time, blood clots in the lungs occur. They may pose a hazard to life. Blood thinners and regular exercise, however, can usually prevent blood clots.
- Occasionally fatal leaks could develop in the new connections made by the weight loss surgery. Five days following surgery, they frequently occur. When you experience symptoms like stomach pain or a cold, you should call your doctor.

You might also observe that your skin is drooping. You might decide to have it removed surgically.

How long will I be hospitalized?

After a laparoscopic gastric bypass and up to four days after an open gastric bypass, the majority of patients stay two days.

How does the distal stomach behave? Does it lessen?

The remnant (or remaining) stomach shrinks with time when it is no longer stretched by food and liquids, but it continues to play a vital role in creating stomach acid and enzymes that aid in food digestion.

What are the dangers of undergoing a gastric bypass?

Your surgeon will go into great depth with you regarding all the hazards associated with this procedure.

After this treatment, will I need to take vitamin supplements?

You won't be able to fulfill the suggested US daily requirements for several vitamins and minerals if they are not absorbed sufficiently. Vitamins B6, B12, folate, calcium, and the mineral iron are examples of this in particular. This is why we insist that you take two multivitamins every day, along with calcium citrate and a dose of vitamin B12 under your tongue once a week for the rest of your life.

What happens if I notice blood in my stool after having a gastric bypass?

Because the treatments to the stomach and intestine will have caused some stress to the tissues, you should expect to see some blood in your stool for the first few bowel movements after surgery. Oozing of a little amount of blood is not unusual. Call your surgeon if this continues or if the toilet water looks to be entirely blood rather than just tinted with blood (appearing like cranberry juice). Go to the closest emergency room if you feel weak or lightheaded. Make sure to inform them that you recently underwent a gastric bypass and to provide the time and name of the surgeon who performed the procedure.

After surgery, how many calories should I consume?

Consume at least 600 calories each day, which will be difficult in the beginning when you don't have an appetite and have a low tolerance for food. Even while this amount of calories might seem absurdly low to you right now, you'll soon learn that on some days in the early postoperative period, it takes work to consume it.

3 DIET BEFORE THE SURGERY

Prior to surgery, you can lower the amount of fat in and around your liver and abdomen by losing weight. As a result, laparoscopy rather than open surgery can be an option for you. Less invasive, requiring less recuperation time, and less taxing on your body are all benefits of laparoscopic surgery. Prior to surgery, you should lose weight to prepare for a new eating style and to keep yourself safer during the process. Your healthcare physician will decide on your precise eating schedule and pre-op weight loss objective with the assistance, most likely, of a qualified dietician. Once you've received the all-clear for the procedure, you can start your dietary regimen. The treatment might be delayed or abandoned if not enough weight is lost. You should begin the diet program as soon as you can for this reason. Individual guidelines will differ, however, they might contain the following:

- Eliminate or cut back on your consumption of foods fried in oil, whole milk products, and fatty meats that are high in saturated fat.
- Eliminate or cut back on your consumption of foods high in carbohydrates, such as pasta, potatoes, bread, bread items, sweet sweets, and spaghetti.
- Juice and sodas and other high-sugar drinks should be avoided.
- Use restraint when consuming.
- Refrain from bingeing.
- Eliminate cigarette smoking.
- Avoid any substances that your doctor has not prescribed.
- Avoid drinking alcohol.
- Avoid drinking anything with your meals.
- regular multivitamin consumption
- consume protein powder or smoothies.

3.1 Food Permitted and food to avoid

Choosing food

Protein shakes and other low-calorie, high-protein foods that are simple to digest make up the majority of the pre-op diet. Muscle tissue is strengthened and protected by protein. This may encourage your body to use fat as fuel rather than muscle. Additionally, protein keeps your body strong, which might hasten recuperation. You might need to stick to a diet that is primarily liquid or liquid-only as your surgery date approaches. Your doctor might allow you to consume some solid foods during this time depending on your weight and general health. These might contain soft-boiled eggs, salmon, or watered-down hot cereal. Prior to the procedure, be sure to confirm the anesthesiologist's instructions regarding what is permitted and prohibited. Depending on your circumstances, these devices might change. For instance, up to two hours prior to surgery, your doctor can advise you to consume drinks high in carbohydrates.

Food to Avoid

- Spicy foods
- Popcorn
- Alcoholic drinks
- Caffeinated drinks
- Breads
- Stale food
- Muffins
- Fast food, hamburgers, chips, fried food, and other fatty stuff.
- Nutty foods
- Stale fruit

4   DIET AFTER THE SURGERY

4.1   What are the phases of the diet?

Following gastric bypass surgery, one must adhere to a strict post-op food program. Your stomach now has a staple line that needs time to heal. The healing process might be hampered by several meals, which can also overwork the staple line and cause a leak. An illustration of post-op food recommendations is provided below. However, the advice given to patients by each surgery center varies slightly. Always heed the recommendations given by the office of your surgeon. There are normally four stages to a post-gastric bypass patient's diet:

- Stage 1: Clear Liquids
- Stage 2: Puree Foods
- Stage 3: Soft Foods
- Stage 4: Solid Foods

Week 1 – Clear Liquids

Following gastric bypass surgery, only clear liquids should be ingested for 1 to 7 days. Keep in mind that the stomach pouch is currently very enlarged and brand-new. To meet your daily fluid objectives, you'll probably need to sip frequently throughout the day. 6 to 8 ounces of fluid should be consumed each waking hour. Your nutritionist will determine the duration of this phase and offer nutritional recommendations. The following components will most likely be included in the clear liquids that the nutritionist suggests:

- Water, herbal tea, fat-free broth, and sugar-free Jell-O (many programs recommend avoiding red-colored Jell-O; this is just a precaution in case you spit up from drinking too fast and saw a bright red color, you or your doctor may think it is blood and rush you for tests)
- Staying hydrated is crucial during this stage. A few days following surgery, some surgeons might advise you to start drinking protein drinks.

Week Two and Three – Pureed Foods

After ingesting clear liquids for one to seven days, you can begin consuming liquefied protein sources. This post-op diet phase often lasts a week (occasionally 2). Due to their smaller stomachs, the patient should take little meals spaced out throughout the day. During the stage 1, You should drink around 64 ounces (about 8 glasses) of clear liquids per day, excluding the liquid in the pureed foods, and consume about 60 to 70 grams of protein per day if you are in stage one of the diet (found in protein shakes, egg whites, and pureed meat or fish).

Processed food.

Beverages with caffeine and carbonation shouldn't be consumed. Simple carbs and refined sugars are to be avoided as well. The sources of pureed protein that are commonly approved by your nutritionist or surgeon are listed below:

- Protein drinks
- Fat-free milk
- Eggs whites
- soft nonfat cheese
- Cottage cheese without fat
- Yogurt high in protein and low in sugar

Straws should not be used when drinking clear liquids since they could introduce unwelcome air into the stomach, which could cause discomfort. Clear liquids should be drunk very slowly. To avoid nutrient deficits, one or two multivitamins per day that contain iron are required. During this time, the multivitamins should be in liquid or chewable form. Additionally, it's crucial to incorporate calcium citrate in your diet; typically, two or three doses with 400 mg to 600 mg each are advised. It is recommended to take supplemental calcium citrate at least two hours apart from multivitamin doses. This is because iron and calcium absorption can conflict, stopping you from absorbing enough for your body needs..

Week 4 and 5 – Soft Foods

At this point in the regimen, you can begin slowly reintroducing soft foods. One to two weeks is a common duration for this stage. Foods that can be easily mashed with a fork or spoon are recommended for stage three of the post-operative gastric bypass diet. Soft meats and cooked vegetables are likely to be part of this diet.

The nutritional objectives will not change from stage two. A daily recommended intake of 64 or more ounces of hydration and 60 or more grams of protein. A protein serving size in stage three should be between 1 and 2 ounces (an ounce is around the size of your thumb), and you should eat between 3 and 6 small meals daily.

Just like stage two, stage three places an emphasis on high-quality lean protein sources. Stage 3 keeps the focus on superior lean protein sources, but it also permits up to three meals of soft vegetables and very little fat (This tiny amount of fat is most likely from one serving of ripe avocados.).

During this phase of the diet, some of the following items will probably be recommended as protein sources:

Eggs, Milk, and Meat

- Fish
- Egg whites
- Skinny chicken
- Lean turkey
- Cottage cheese without fat
- Tofu
- Cheese without the fat

Vegetables

- Carrots
- Avocados
- Potatoes
- Bananas
- Green beans
- Tomatoes
- Cucumbers
- Squash

You still need two or three doses of calcium citrate of 400-600 mg each, taken at least two hours apart and separate from the multivitamin. Your nutritionist may advise you to take 3,000 IU of vitamin D3 per day, which you will most likely find in a multivitamin designed specifically for calcium and bariatrics. It is crucial to take at least 350 mcg of vitamin B12 and 12 mg of thiamin daily; fortunately, these dosages are included in the majority of bariatric-specific multivitamins.

Week 6 – Solid Foods

Solid food has returned! Now that you've made it this far, it's time to start eating actual food. At this point, it is critical to practice mindful eating. Make sure you sit down and pay attention to how your body feels during each meal. Set a timer and finish your meal in no more than 20 minutes by taking little, dime-sized bites, setting your fork down in between bites, and chewing your food until it resembles applesauce before swallowing.

For the remainder of your life, have a diet high in protein, vegetables, minimal amounts of carbohydrates, and little to no refined sweets.

Advice for introducing solid foods:

- Ideally, only one new food should be consumed once each day so you can track how your body reacts to it.
- Eat gradually. Give each bite 15 seconds of careful chewing. Utilize the Baritastic app's timer.
- Space out your meals and liquids by at least 30 minutes.
- Maintain your daily water intake of at least 64 ounces.
- Eat your protein first, followed by your vegetables, and then your carbohydrates—ideally, whole grains or fruits, not processed foods—in that order.

When sugary and/or fatty foods are ingested too rapidly or in excess, dumping syndrome develops. The stomach forces a meal before it enters the small intestine can be thoroughly digested. Dumping syndrome typically causes vomiting, diarrhea, nausea, sweating, cramps, a rise in heart rate, etc, these side effects often subside after one to two hours. However, "dumping" is a highly terrible experience, therefore you should avoid it.

To lessen the danger of dumping

- Avoid foods with a lot of sugar or refined carbs.
- Consume food slowly.
- Take your time chewing.

Food to avoid

- Grapes,
- Almonds,
- Shellfish
- Meat,
- Pork,

- Whole grains.
- Pineapple
- Salad with corn beans and lettuce
- Asparagus

5 NUTRITIONAL EXPECTATIONS AND REQUIREMENTS

It is expected that after the bariatric surgery, that you would have to make some adjustments in the way that you eat. As with all post-operative expectations, you would begin with a full liquid diet – soups and gelatin among others, as your body gradually transitions from its customary eating habits to one that accommodates the new adjustments that took place with the occurrence of your surgical procedure. You will have to accustom yourself to several practices that your physician may prescribe:

- Eat and drink slowly- we have mentioned about the effects of dumping syndrome earlier – an expected side effect with bariatric procedures. Take your time when you consume your small, frequent meals. 30 minutes is usually a good place to start.
- Small, frequent meals – You will not hear enough of this, so make this your principle for meal planning. Ideally, start off with six small meals a day, then gradually lessen these to four meals a day, then acclimatize your body to three meals a day.
- Frequently hydrate – 8 cups of water is a constant measure for the adequate amount of fluids you must take. Take care to monitor your fluid consumption however, as this could fool your stomach into thinking that it is fuller than it actually is, and deprive you of nutrients that you would have been able to consume instead. Additionally, the fluids that should be consumed here can be water, or even soups. Caffeinated and sugary drinks are not good fluid substitutes due to their high sugar content.

- Thorough Chewing – remember that bariatric surgery has modified the structure of your stomach, so it can no longer accommodate larger chunks of food. Because the opening to the stomach has been narrowed, large chunks of food can potentially block this passageway. As a result, your stomach may not receive the food it needs, and this can cause you to suffer from nausea and vomiting, as well as from pain in your abdomen. This time, act like food processor and reduce your food into the finest consistency to make it easier for your body to handle.

- High-Protein, High-Priority – the base of your meals should be high in protein, as this form of surgery does not lend itself well to the consumption of carbohydrates. Foods with high protein content should be consumed first, to ease the transition process for your body.

- High-Fat, High-Sugar, High-Time to Avoid – foods laden with fat or prepared with fat and with a high sugar content – refined sugars to be precise – are to be avoided. This would significantly trigger the effects of dumping syndrome by your body. This does not mean however that desserts are taboo, as you can still have your cake and eat it! Just pay attention to the ingredients that went into your desserts, or simply flip through the pages of this book for a suitable snack that you can nosh on.

- Listen to your Stomach – your stomach has a built-in signal to stop you from eating. Because it is now smaller in structure, it can rapidly signal your body to stop eating. Feel for this signal, and resist the impulse to stuff one more bite. Your body and weight-loss journey will thank you.

Now that we have established the types of adjustments you would have to do to ensure that you optimize the effects of bariatric surgery, we delve into the types of food items that you are allowed to consume. Remember, now that your stomach has been fundamentally altered, so has the types of food that you can now consume. What you eat will have a lasting effect on your body, and it is important to know what you can eat to ensure that you remain on track with your weight loss journey.

- **Liquids** – earlier we mentioned that hydration is an important factor in the success of your weight-loss journey. This helps prevent the occurrence of dehydration – an easily preventable post-operative condition. However, you cannot consume liquids with your meals, or consume any form of liquid 30 minutes before and after you eat. To ensure that you remain adequately hydrated, always carry a bottle of water with you as it is the safest liquid that you can drink at any time. Consume small amounts frequently – don't chug, your stomach will not let you.
    o To Drink: Water, Milk, Soy Milk, Protein Shakes, Decaf Tea and Coffee (without any Cream, Creamer or Sugar), Sugar-Free Drinks, and those liquids that are not carbonated (No Sodas, or Seltzers either).
    o To Avoid: Juices (especially the artificially sweetened ones), Caffeinated Drinks (Sodas, Coffee, Tea, and Energy Drinks), Carbonated Water, any sugary drinks Alcoholic Drinks, Sports Drinks, Sweet Tea, and Lemonade.
    o Ideal Amount: 8 cups of water gradually increased as you heal from the post-operative stage.

- **Proteins** – Protein is an essential nutrient for all post-operative patients as this helps the body repair the tissues that were cut into in the operation. Low-carb and low-calorie diets need that you eat a sufficient quantity of protein to maintain muscle mass while your body eliminates the extra fat, and this also serves to keep your body pleased longer. Our body generally digests proteins a lot slower than it does carbohydrates. Aside from its importance in the recovery process of the body post-operatively, the consumption of protein allows the body to maintain its weight loss trajectory, for a longer period of time.
    o To Eat: Eggs, Skinless Poultry, Chicken or Turkey Sausage (without any nitrates or preservatives), All Seafood, Low-Fat and Non-Fat Dairy Items such as low-fat cottage cheese, nonfat milk and cheese, lean beef (if your body allows for it) but only after three months after the operation, this can include the following cuts such as sirloin, loin, round roasts, or steak. Ground beef may be used only in its leanest forms, lean

pork may be eaten three months after the operation, specifically the tenderloin, top loin, the chops and ham – with the fat from the ham trimmed. Vegetarian proteins such as tofu, lentils, beans, nuts and seeds are welcome substitutes.

- o Not to Eat: Whole Milk and Cream as these are high-fat dairy products, cuts of beef and pork that are high in fat – pay close attention to the marbling of the beef particularly – these may seem low in fat, but most of the fat is located in between the muscle of the meat, preserved pork products such as sausage, bacon, bologna, and pork ribs, ground beef (except if it is lean as provided earlier), and poultry cuts with their skin.
- o Portions: Up to a hundred grams per serving (roughly the size of your palm), but specific recommendations are dependent upon your body type, as well as the number of days since your operation,

- **Carbohydrates** – are the basic nutrients that the body uses to fuel its metabolic processes. However, immediately after the surgical procedure, you consume little to no carbs, where the body will utilize its fat stores as the energy source needed for it to function. Carbohydrates can have either a simple or complicated structure: Simple carbohydrates are sugars that are easily absorbed by the body and provide an immediate source of energy. Complex carbohydrates comprise starches, and are slowly digested by the body to provide an energy source of sufficient duration. To differentiate in terms of food: Simple Carbohydrates include items like sodas, fruit juices, and items made with refined white flour. Complex carbohydrates tend to be high in fiber content, and are often food items made with whole-grains, as well as fruits and vegetables. As a rule, avoid the simple, and opt for the more complex carbohydrates.
  - o To Eat: Fresh Fruits, Vegetables, Sweet Potatoes, Potatoes with Skin, Oatmeal, Whole-Grain Products to include Bread, Pasta – ideally toasted whole grains, Wild and Brown Rice, and Ancient Grains (Quinoa, Barley, Spelt, Millet, Faro and Amaranth).
  - o To Avoid: Products made from refined white flour, fruit juices, soda and potato chips.
  - o Portions: Small amount immediately after the operation, later increased over time to accommodate carbohydrates as a larger part of the meal.

- **Fats** – Dietary fats are essential for the body so it can metabolize certain vitamins. Retinol, Phylloquinone, Tocopherol and Phytonadione are called fat-soluble vitamins and can only be absorbed and used with the presence of fats. Some fatty acids cannot be created by the body, so we have to consume other foods to be able to get these fatty acids. Fats are calorie-rich foods, and therefore, care must be taken that we consume only the amount that the body needs, regardless of the nutritional value of the fats. Read the labels of food items carefully as some fat-free items may have no fat, but substitute it with additives to make up for the flavor that was lost. With dairy products, look for low fat options such as milk, yogurt and cottage cheese that can save you the extra calories and skimp on the saturated fats.
  - o To Eat: Avocados, Chia Seeds, Fatty Fish such as Salmon, Seafood and Shellfish, Flax and Flaxseed, Extra-Virgin Olive Oil, Almonds, Walnuts, Peanuts and other Nut Butters.
  - o To Use Cautiously: Butter, Palm and Coconut Oils, Whole-Fat Dairy, and other Vegetable Oils.
  - o To Avoid: Animal Fats (Beef Tallow, Lard), Fried Items, Trans-fats, Foods prepared with Saturated Fat.
  - o Portions: Initially small quantities, and must comprise less than 30 percent of your meal if you use healthier fats, 7 percent or less of the meal if you used animal fats.

- **Supplements** – Vitamin and Mineral Supplements can boost the functions of your body and augment its nutrient supply as your body begins to adjust to its new state. It is advisable though that you consume your supplements with food as some components of these supplements are readily absorbed with food. When you do this, it is perfectly fine to take some water with it. It helps the vitamin go down easily. Be sure to avoid the gumdrop version of vitamins however, as these tend to be sugar-laden and often lack the vitamins in quantities needed by the body.

- o Multivitamins are a good idea, to ensure that you do obtain the needed vitamin requirements of your body. Try to obtain more than what your body needs. This often requires you to take two vitamin tablets in two separate doses.
- o Vitamin D is always a great idea, as most patients who undergo bariatric surgery often lack this vitamin. Vitamin D levels however, are dependent upon your body's needs and will require consultation with a nutritionist and a physician.
- o Calcium is always a needed supplement because of its role in the promotion of bone health. Calcium needs may range up to 1500 mg per day in several doses.
- o Iron is needed by the body to produce erythrocytes, cells that carry oxygen and nutrients to all the parts of the body. While not a traditional supplement prescribed to those who have undergone bariatric surgery, your need for iron will depend upon the levels that your body has.
- o Vitamin B12 (Cobalamin) is an important vitamin that must be considered as part of your supplementation as a deficiency of this vitamin can lead to pernicious anemia, a lifelong condition that requires supplementation with this vitamin. This vitamin also helps enhance your nerve function. Your Vitamin B12 levels will need to be checked to ensure that you do receive nutritionally adequate amounts.

Conclusion

Your weight loss journey with the help of bariatric surgery requires commitment from you, and support from your loved ones who would take the journey alongside you – an important part of your recovery process as well as your journey to better yourself. From the pages that can be gleaned here, you can see that though you would be cutting off some of the usual food items we encounter, there are still ways to prepare food items that are good for you, without the side effects of weight gain and dumping syndrome among other conditions. The next chapter will discuss the various ingredient substitutions that you can make in your pantry to ensure that you get the best effects from your bariatric surgery. It may take some getting used to, but keep your endgame in sight: You're doing this to live a healthier life, for yourself, and your loved ones. For now, let's get your pantry reorganized, and go out with the old, and in with the new items.

6 PREPARATIONS FOR COOKERY

Cookery Techniques Needed

There are certain food preparations that must be considered before you begin cooking, but a certainty is that you definitely cannot have anything deep-fried in fat. If you do have an air-fryer however, that would be an ideal substitute, as you can have your guilt-free, fat-free, fried food and eat it. Generally however, even when you do eat out, a good rule of thumb to live by is to opt for food preparations that require little to no fat in the techniques. This includes the use of steamed options as the best, along with poached, and boiled items, sautéed items are fine provided you use healthier fats. If you do not have an air fryer, consider other alternatives such as baking, roasting and grilling, you never know which techniques to consider until you try them. This book would guide you into cooking in ways that you would normally never consider. All it takes is some guidance and a lot of creativity.

Prepare Your Pantry

There are certain substitutions that must be made in your pantry especially with your staple items. It would be best to check off the items in this list as we go along and prepare you for a well-stocked pantry that would help you prepare the meal of your dreams.

Original Ingredient	Substitute
Vegetable Oil	Extra-Virgin Olive Oil
All-Purpose Flour	Whole-Wheat Pastry Flour
Sour Cream	Low-Fat, Plain Greek Yogurt, Hummus
Processed Cheese and Cheese Spreads	Cheeses such as Mozzarella, Feta, Ricotta and Cottage Cheese
Pre-Made, Canned Soups	Dried Beans, Canned Beans and Low-Sodium Chicken Stock
Hotdogs, Bacon	Nitrate-free Lean Turkey or Chicken Sausage
Instant Oatmeal	Old-Style Steel Cut or Rolled Oats
Fruit Snacks	Fresh Fruit, Natural, Unsweetened Applesauce, Frozen Fruit, Fruit Cups in Water or Natural Juice
Processed and Preserved Meats	Nitrate-free, Deli-Sliced Turkey, Lean Roast Beef, Ham and Chicken.
Juice	Water infused with Lemon and Lime Slices and Herbal Teas
Potato Chips and other salted snack items	Dehydrated Vegetables and Snap Peas, Kale Chips
Regular Yogurt with Flavorings	Plain yogurt, Low-Sugar Greek Yogurt
Canned Meats	Canned Chicken Breast, Shrimp, Tuna, Salmon or Crab
Pasta	Spaghetti Squash, Courgette Ribbons, or Whole-Grain Pasta
Pre-made Salad Dressings	Infused Vinegars with Extra-Virgin Olive Oil, Yogurt-Based Salad Dressings

There are some items that you can make from scratch such as your very own snack items, as well as a few condiments and dressings that you not only help you on your weight-loss journey, but help you economize on food costs in the long run. Besides, knowing how to whip up a few salad dressings and snacks for instance can impress any guests you may have in your home. Another important step bariatric surgery cookery is the need to count protein portions, especially since this will be the main source of energy of your body for most of the recovery process. Additionally, when you are able to determine how much protein you will actually need to consume, you will be able to manage the amount of weight you lose better.

Food Item	Portion Size	Protein/ Gram
Poultry, Beef, Pork and Fish	2 ounces	14 grams of protein, with 7 grams in each ounce.
Shrimps and Scallops	15 large pieces (3 ounces)	18 grams of protein
Luncheon Meat (Nitrate-Free, Deli-Sliced Turkey, Chicken, Ham and Roast Beef)	2 ounces (Approximately 4-6 thin slices)	10 grams
Eggs	1 large	7 grams
Egg Whites	From 2 large eggs	8 grams
Cottage or Ricotta Cheese (Fat-Free or 1-2% Fat)	Half a cup	14 grams
Mozzarella, Cheddar, Colby, Feta	1 slice	7 grams
Non-Fat or Low-Fat Greek Yogurt	¾ cup	10-15 grams
Non-Fat or Low-Fat Regular Yogurt	¾ cup	5 grams
Lentils and Pulses	½ cup cooked lentils	9 grams
Beans	½ cup cooked beans	5-9 grams

Once you have determined the portion sizes, and the ingredients that you would need for your pantry, the most important items are the kitchen equipment that you will use to prepare the recipes in this cookbook. Immersion Blenders and Hand Blenders are used in the preparation of finely-textured soups and sauces, and are also useful in the preparation of chili con carne and other dishes that require the food to be fine in texture, or pureed. The convenience with the use of the immersion blender is that you can use this on the stovetop, although you will need to take the usual kitchen precautions. Spiralizers are a handy tool if you would like to make your own vegetable noodles from scratch. Spiralizers are best used to make courgette noodles, earlier mentioned as a superb pasta substitute. For your kitchen, opt for a smaller version that you can keep on your kitchen counter. Muffin Tins are great if you would like to learn how to control your portions. There are two types of muffin tins however, regular sized and mini muffin tins. These also serve as a popular mold for baked egg recipes for your own egg muffins. Blenders or Food Processors are often described as the kitchen workhorse, and will have the same functionalities here. Some of these recipes would involve the use of the blender to make your own protein-rich smoothies, and the food processor with each attachment could ease the amount of preparations you need for the ingredients in these recipes. Use the food processor and blender suitable for your needs. There are numerous blenders for instance that allow you to do a single-serving of smoothies. Be sure however, to not overload your blender or food processor so as to not let the motor overheat. Add ingredients gradually, to ensure that your products remain consistent. Smaller blenders will have smaller motors so be sure to gauge your blenders and food processors functional capacity. Slow-Cookers, particularly the five-quart size are another kitchen workhorse as they allow you to cook meat slowly while it retains the moisture. There are smaller or larger versions of the slow cooker, be sure to purchase according to your needs. Vegetable Peelers do a great job in the removal of the protective peels of fruits and vegetables. This is an integral piece of equipment, especially in the earlier days of your post-operative experience. Air-Fryers are the answer to all your fried food cravings as this allows you to enjoy fried items, without all the added fat you get from the use of conventional frying methods. If you do enjoy fried food (who doesn't?), the air fryer would be a worthwhile investment in your kitchen. Before you use this however, be sure to use Extra-virgin olive oil spray on the food items to be fried to retain the crispy texture associated with our favorite fried items.

7 STAGE 1 - CLEAR LIQUID DIET

The clear liquid diet is often the first stage of diet for those who have newly undergone bariatric surgery. You would find that for those who have newly undergone surgery, it is standard that they be placed on a clear liquid diet as the body begins to adjust itself to accommodate foods. For those who have undergone bariatric surgery however, not only does the body have to adjust from all the surgery and anesthesia, but also the reduction in the capacity of your stomach. A clear liquid diet allows your body to gradually adjust to a limited capacity and absorb the nutrients that it needs to sustain itself. Recipes under this section include the presence of broths and popsicles as these are the foods that your body would be able to tolerate in its post-operative stage.

8 BROTHS

8.1 Bone Stock

Prep Time: 1 hr. Cook Time: 12 hrs. Serves: 12 cups in 1 cup portions

Ingredients:

- 2 pounds beef bones (ideally joints and knuckles)
- one gallon water
- two tbsp apple-cider vinegar
- one onion, minced
- two big carrots, minced
- 2 celery-stalks, minced
- 1 tbsp. salt
- 1 tsp. peppercorns
- 1 bunch fresh parsley (or herbs of your choosing)
- 2 garlic cloves

Procedure:

1. Set the oven temperature to 400 degrees Fahrenheit. Roast the bones on a baking pan for 30 minutes. Allow the roasted bones, together with the water & vinegar, to settle for 30 min in a stock pot. Stir periodically until the onions, carrots, and celery come to a boil.

2. In a slow cooker, combine the bones, stock, and mirepoix (diced vegetables), together with the salt and peppercorns. Cook on lower temp for 12 to 24 hours, skimming any contaminants that float to the surface with a spoon.

3. Herbs and garlic should be added during the last 30 minutes of cooking. Remove the pan from the heat and place it on a cooling rack. Utilize a fine-mesh metal strainer. Once the stock has cooled, remove the fat by skimming.

4. Transfer the stock into air-tight jars. Store inside a fridge for as long as 5 days or inside a freezer for as long as 3 months.

Nutritional Value: Calories: 69, Fat: 4g, Carbohydrates: 1g, Protein: 6g, Fiber: 0g, Sugar: 0g, Sodium: 581mg

8.2 Chicken Broth *

Preparation Time: 15 minutes Cooking Time: 2 hours and 30 minutes Serves: 4 in 1 cup portions.

Ingredients:

- Onion, two medium sized pieces, diced
- Carrots, two medium sized pieces, diced
- Celery, 1 rib cut into chunks
- Thyme, 1 teaspoon, dried
- Rosemary, 1 teaspoon, dried
- Bone-in Chicken, 1 two-pound bird
- Salt to taste
- Water, 2 cups (start with hot)

Procedure:

1. Prepare the mirepoix base for the broth. Once this has been prepared, add all of the ingredients into the bottom of a deep pan. Bring the pan to a boil.
2. It is expected that foam will form on top of the boiling mixture. Skim the foam and discard it. If you find this difficult to do, you may add some egg white to solidify the foam. This makes it easier for you to skim, and also helps make your broth clearer. Once all the foam has been skimmed off, cover the pan and allow to simmer for two hours and thirty minutes on low heat.
3. Remove the solids from the soup and set aside, you will only want the broth. Use the mirepoix and chicken meat for other purposes. Season your soup to taste.
4. Serve hot or at room temperature if preferred.

Nutritional Value: Calories: 378, Fat: 3.5g, Carbohydrates: 58.4g, Protein: 30g, Fiber: 15.1g, Sugar: 27g, Sodium: 2638mg Cholesterol: 72mg

8.3 Cannellini and Bone Broth*

Preparation Time: 10 minutes Cooking Time: 40 minutes. Serves: 4 in 1 cup portions.

Ingredients:

- Olive Oil, Extra-Virgin, 1 tablespoon
- Zucchini, small, 1 piece, diced
- Carrot, small, 1 piece, diced
- Onion, 1 medium-sized piece, chopped
- Tomatoes, 4 medium-sized pieces, chopped and seeded.
- Garlic, 4 cloves, minced
- Spinach, 1 bunch, washed
- Cannellini Beans, 1 cup, pre-soaked
- Chicken Bone Broth, 2 cups
- Cayenne Pepper, 1 pinch
- Thyme, 1 teaspoon, dried
- Parsley, ¼ cup, chopped
- Basil, ¼ cup, chopped
- Beef Gelatine dissolved in water, 2 tablespoons
- Parmesan Cheese to taste
- Salt to taste

Procedure:

1. In a deep pan, heat the oil over medium heat. Once heated, sauté the onion until it becomes fragrant and translucent. Add the minced garlic and cook until golden. Add all of the spices into the pan next along with the diced carrots and cook for another minute.
2. Add the zucchini and tomatoes into the pan and cook for another minute. Add the beans and pour in the bone broth. Allow to simmer for a few more minutes.
3. Add the herbs and season with the parmesan cheese and salt to your preference. Allow to simmer for one more minute and ladle this into bowls and serve warm.

Nutritional Value: Calories: 1186, Fat: 20g, Carbohydrates: 176.7g, Protein: 93.8g, Fiber: 65.8g, Sugar: 29.2g, Sodium: 3946mg Cholesterol: 4mg

8.4 Basic Beef Bone Broth*

Preparation Time: 5 minutes. Cooking Time: 8 hours. Serves: 8, portioned into 2 tablespoons

Ingredients:

- Cooking Spray
- Yellow Onion, 1 medium-sized piece, chopped
- Celery, 1 cup, diced
- Carrot, 1 cup, diced
- Beef Bones, 3 pounds
- Stewing Beef, 1 pound
- Water, 12 cups
- Salt, 1 teaspoon
- Bay Leaves, 2 pieces
- Garlic, 1 tablespoon, minced

Procedure:

1. Preheat an oven to 400 degrees Fahrenheit. Spray a shallow roasting pan with the cooking spray and set aside.
2. Arrange the onions, carrots and celery in an even layer at the bottom of the prepared roasting pan. Arrange the beef bones and the stewing beef on top of the vegetables and roast in the preheated oven for 40 minutes, turning the bones, meat and vegetables over after twenty minutes of roasting.
3. Remove the roasting pan from the oven with oven mitts and tip the contents into a large stock pot. Add the water, salt, bay leaves and the minced garlic cloves and bring the mixture to a boil. Stir frequently to prevent sticking at the bottom of the pot.
4. Lower the heat to a low flame and allow the broth to simmer for at least four hours. Stir every hour. You may allow the broth to simmer for up to eight hours for a more flavorful result.
5. With the aid of a kitchen spider, remove the bones, meat and vegetables from the broth. Serve warm.

Nutritional Value: Calories: 495, Fat: 16.9g, Carbohydrates: 31.3g, Protein: 52.6g, Fiber: 8.3g, Sugar: 12.4g, Sodium: 2712mg Cholesterol: 126mg

8.5 Clear Vegetable Broth*

Preparation Time: 10 minutes Cooking Time: 18 minutes. Serves: 4 in 1 cup portions

Ingredients:

- Carrots, 1 cup, diced
- Onions, 1 cup, diced
- Tomato Paste, two tablespoons
- Cabbage, 4 cups, chopped
- Green Beans, 1 cup, trimmed and string removed
- Garlic, two cloves, minced
- Bell Peppers, two small pieces, chopped
- Beef Broth, 4 cups (see recipe in this chapter)
- Zucchini, 1 cup, chopped
- Broccoli, 1 cup, chopped
- Bay Leaves, 2 pieces, torn
- Thyme, dried, ½ teaspoon
- Basil, dried, ½ teaspoon
- Salt and Pepper to taste
- Olive Oil to sauté

Procedure:

1. In a stockpot, sauté the carrots and onions in oil until they have softened. Add the cabbage and the green beans and cook for an additional five minutes.
2. Add the remainder of the ingredients and bring the mixture to a boil. Lower the heat and allow the mixture to simmer for 15-20 minutes. Remove the bay leaves from the soup.
3. You may strain the vegetables for a clear broth and serve warm.

Nutritional Value: Calories: 527, Fat: 15.9g, Carbohydrates: 92.4g, Protein: 17.7g, Fiber: 28.5g, Sugar: 37.4g, Sodium: 6174mg Cholesterol: 0mg

9 POPSICLES AND SORBETS

9.1 Tropical Popsicles

Prep Time: 10 mins. Serves: 2

Ingredients:

- 1 Half cups unsweetened orange juice
- 2 ripe bananas
- 2 ripe mangoes

Procedure:

1. Bananas are peeled and then cut into bits. Put into a blender. Peel and dice the mangoes before placing them in a blender. Orange juice should be poured over the fruit. mix until homogenous. The mixture is poured into four Popsicle molds and frozen until hardened.

Nutritional Value: Calories: 770, Fat: 3.9g, Carb: 191.4g, Protein: 10.3g, Fiber: 17.6g, Sugar: 152g, Sodium: 17mg

9.2 Protein Packed Milk*

Preparation Time: 5 minutes Cooking Time: 0

Serves: 4 in 1 cup portions

Ingredients:

- Skim Milk, 4 cups
- Non-fat Milk, Dried and Powdered, 1 cup

Procedure:

1. In a bowl or a blender jar, add the skim milk and powdered non-fat milk and blend until well incorporated. Store in an airtight container and keep refrigerated. Use within a week and discard any left overs. Use as you would milk.

Nutritional Value: Calories: 440, Fat: 0g, Carbohydrates: 59g, Protein: 39g, Fiber: 0g, Sugar: 59g, Sodium: 630mg

9.3 Chocolate Pudding Popsicles

Prep Time: 5 mins + 4 hrs. to freeze

Serves: 2

Ingredients:

- one (3.9-ounce) package chocolate-flavored instant pudding
- 2 cups cold low-fat milk
- two scoops chocolate protein powder

Procedure:

1. In a small bowl, whisk the milk, protein powder, and pudding mix for at least two minutes. Fill ice pop molds or paper cups with mixture. Insert a Popsicle stick into each mold's center. Refrigerate for 4 hours, or until firm. Unform before serving.

Nutritional Value: Calories: 215, Fat: 2g, Carbohydrates: 36g, Protein: 12g, Fiber: 0g, Sugar: 27g, Sodium: 480mg.

9.4 Citrus Mousse

Prep Time: 15 mins + 4 hrs. to chill Serves: 2 in 1 cup portions

Ingredients:

- 1Half cups simmering water
- Fresh fruit, for serving
- 1Half cups whipped topping
- 2 cups ice cubes
- one (six-ounce) pkg sugarless lemon-flavored gelatin

Procedure:

1. Mix the boiling water and gelatin in a big microwave - safe basin and whisk until fully dissolved. Mix for at least two minutes to completely dissolve the gelatin. Dissolve the ice cubes by stirring them in. 5 to 10 minutes in the fridge until thickened.

2. Fold in the whipped topping. Divide into four portions and refrigerate until firm, about 4 hours. Garnish with fresh fruit before serving

Nutritional Value: Calories: 85, Fat: 6g, Carbohydrates: 6g, Protein: 1g, Fiber: 0g, Sugar: 3g, Sodium: 45mg.

9.5 Fresh Strawberry Smoothie*

Preparation Time: 5 minutes Cooking Time: 0

Serves: 1

Ingredients:

- Non-fat, Plain Greek Yogurt, 1 cup
- Strawberries, Unsweetened, Frozen, 1 cup
- Stevia Extract, ¼ teaspoon

Procedure:

1. Add all of the ingredients to a blender jar and blend on a low setting until thoroughly combined. If you prefer a thinner product, you may add a few tablespoons of almond milk until it reaches your desired consistency. Pour into a glass and serve.

Nutritional Value: Calories: 207, Fat: 0.2g, Carbohydrates: 41.2g, Protein: 13g, Fiber: 7.6g, Sugar: 28.1g, Sodium: 184mg, Cholesterol: 5mg

9.6 Watermelon and Basil Granita

Prep Time: 10 mins + 3-4 hrs to Chill Serves: 4 in ½ cup portions

Ingredients:

- fresh basil leaves, finely chopped, ¼ cup
- 1 cup watermelon, peel removed, roughly chopped
- Juice of Half lime

- sugar (or sugar substitute), 2 tbsps.

Procedure:

1. Juice of one lime and sugar (if using) should be blended with the watermelon chunks. Blend to a creamy texture by increasing the speed to high. Toss the basil leaves in mixture and place it in a nine-by-thirteen-inch baking dish. One hour inside a freezer.

2. Using a fork, scrape the frozen surfaces until they are broken up entirely. Repeat this process every half hour for at least two to three hours, or until the granite resembles gritty ice. Before serving, scrape the surface with a razor blade.

Nutritional Value: Calories: 76, Fat: 0g, Carbohydrates: 20g, Protein: 1g, Fiber: 1g, Sugar: 16g, Sodium: 2mg.

9.7 Lemon and Blackberry Fro-Yo

Prep Time: 10 mins. Serves: 1

Ingredients:

- 2/3 cup frozen blackberries
- Juice of Half lemon
- Half tsp. liquid stevia
- ¼ cup no fat plain Greek yogurt
- new mint leaves, for sprinkling

Procedure:

1. In a mixer, add all the contents except the mint. mix until homogeneous, about 5 minutes. preserve in tight jar for as long as 3 weeks.

Nutritional Value: Calories: 68, Fat: 0g, Carb: 15g, Protein: 3g, Fiber: 5g, Sugar: 11g, Sodium: 12mg

10 STAGE 2 - PUREED FOOD PHASE and FULL LIQUID DIET

There are two progressions that may take place after the clear liquid diet. This is dependent on the ability of your stomach to tolerate the variety of food that is available. If you feel that your stomach needs more time to adjust to food, then you can stick with a full liquid diet that consists of more substantial soups for your lunch and dinner. If you feel that you are able to tolerate food that is of a heavier consistency, then you may progress to the pureed food phase, which includes not only recipes that have been subjected to a blender, but also those that have been sufficiently mashed with a fork.

11 SOUPS and PUREES

11.1 Split Pea Soup

Prep Time: 10 mins. Cook Time: 1 hr 10 mins.
Serves: 1 gallon in 1 cup portions
Ingredients:
- Extra-virgin olive oil, one tbsp.
- minced two large carrots
- one diced medium onion,
- two , minced garlic cloves
- chicken stock, four cups
- 2 cups water
- Salt
- Fresh powder black pepper
- two dried bay leaves
- one (16-ounce) bag green split peas

Procedure:
1. In a large stockpot, heat the oil over medium heat. Garlic, carrots, and onion should be cooked for about five minutes, or until soft. After adding the stock and water, season with peppercorns. The bay leaves and split peas should be combined in a large mixing dish. Bring to a simmer while continually stirring.
2. Lower the heat to low, cover, and cook for 60 min, or when the peas become tender. Take off bay leaves and serve right away.

Nutritional Value: Calories: 92, Fat: 1g, Carbohydrates: 20g, Protein: 8g, Fiber: 8g, Sugar: 2g, Sodium: 264mg

11.2 Creamed Broccoli Chowder

Prep Time: 20 mins. Cook Time: 1 -1 ½ hrs.
Serves: 10 cups in 1 cup portions
Ingredients:
- olive oil, three tbsps.
- Butter, three tbsps.
- One diced sweet onion,
- Two shredded carrots,
- Flour, five tbsps.
- one tsp. Salt
- Half tsp. nutmeg
- half tsp. Black-pepper
- fat-free divided OR milk three cups
- chicken stock or two cups bone stock 1 15-ounce can (see recipe under this section)
- six cups chopped broccoli
- shredded cheddar cheese one Half cups (optional)

Procedure:
3. In a big stockpot, warm the oil and butter. Sauté the carrots and onion gradually over moderate flame until the onions are soft. Mix in the flour and spices until the flour is completely transparent. Add the milk or half-and-half, chicken stock, and broccoli to the pot. Boil, swirling occasionally, for approximately 1-1/2 hrs over low heat. If using, sprinkle with cheese immediately before dishing.

Nutritional Value: Calories: 199 Fat: 9g Carb: 26g, Protein: 4g, Fiber: 1g, Sugar: 5g, Sodium: 249 mg

11.3 Black Bean Soup

Prep and Cook Time: 20 mins. Serves: 4 cups in 1 cup portions

Ingredients:

- Shredded Cheddar, minced cilantro, and slices of green onions
- low-fat sour cream - 1/4 cup
- Kosher salt and fresh ground black pepper
- mild roasted tomato sauce - ¼ cup
- Chicken Stock or low-salt chicken stock - 1/2 cup
- black beans - 1/2 of 15 ounce can washed and dry
- garlic clove, minced
- small onion one, minced

Procedure:

1. Heat the oil in a large, heavy skillet over medium temperature. Cook for approximately 4 minutes, or until the onion and garlic are lightly browned but not burnt. Season with salt and pepper the beans, stock, and salsa.
2. Bring the soup to a simmer, then lower to a low heat and simmer for 10 minutes, stirring occasionally, until the flavours have melded and the soup has thickened somewhat.
3. In a blender or with an immersion mixer, puree the soup until creamy & smooth. Because steam swells the contents of hot liquids, always cover the lid with a kitchen towel. Pulse the trigger before mixing, then release the vapor.
4. Warm up the soup just before serving and mix in the soured cream. sprinkle sodium chloride to taste. Serve the soup in dishes with cheese, cilantro, and green onions on top.

Nutritional Value: Calories: 701, Fat: 21.8g, Carbs: 75.9g, Protein: 52.3g, Fiber: 17.5g, Sugar: 7.1g, Sodium: 1381mg

11.4 Gazpacho

Prep Time: 10 mins. Serves: 4 cups in 1 ¼ cup portions

Ingredients:

- ripe tomatoes, six Large peeled and seeded
- coarsely crushed onion, Half cup
- chopped seeded peeled cucumber, Half cup
- coarsely cut (green) capsicum, Half cup
- one chopped clove garlic,
- low-sodium tomato juice, one cup
- one tsp. lemon juice
- Black-pepper, 1/eight tsp.
- Hot-pepper salsa, 1/eight tsp.
- no-fat yogurt

Procedure:

1. In a blender or blender, mix tomatoes, capsicum, cucumber, onion, and garlic. Pulse the ingredients until it is thick. Place in a small mixing basin.
2. mix the hot pepper sauce, lemon juice, black pepper, and tomato juice in a mixing bowl. Refrigerate until ready to serve. Start serving with a dollop of low fat yogurt on top.

Nutritional Value: Calories: 68, Fat: 1g, Carbohydrate: 15g, Protein 3g, Fiber 4g, Sugars: 11g, Sodium 25 mg

11.5 Roasted Carrot and Ginger Soup

Prep Time: 15 mins. Cook Time: 45 mins. Serves: 4 cups in 1 cup portions

Ingredients:

- 1 lb. (1kg) baby carrots
- Olive oil, 1 tbsp. divided
- salt, Half tsp. divided
- black pepper, Half tsp. freshly ground, divided
- 1 small yellow onion, diced
- 1 minced clove garlic,
- Grated fresh ginger , 1 tbsp.
- low-sodium vegetable stock, 2 cups divided

- Half tsp. freshly squeezed lemon juice
- Coconut milk(optional), to serve
- scallions(optional), to garnish

Procedure:
1. Prepare oven at 400 degree F
2. Toss the carrots with half a tablespoon of olive oil, 14 teaspoons of salt, and 14 teaspoons of pepper in a large mixing bowl. Arrange the carrots in a single layer on the baking sheet that has been prepared. Bake for 30 minutes or until golden brown after preheating the oven to 350 degrees Fahrenheit.
3. In a large saucepan, heat the remaining half tablespoon of olive oil over medium heat. As soon as the pan is heated, add the onion and a touch of salt. Cook for 5 to 7 minutes, stirring intermittently, or until transparent. Cook for 30 seconds, or until the perfume of the garlic and ginger is released.
4. Place the roasted carrots, sautéed onion and garlic, and 2 to 3 cups vegetable stock in a blender. Blend on high until the mixture is smooth and creamy. Add the carrot purée to a large stock pot. Stir in the remaining 12–2 cup stock and the lemon juice until everything is well combined. Cook for 10 minutes over low heat, uncovered. Stir once in a while. To taste, season with the remaining ½ tsp salt and 1/2 tsp pepper. Serve warm with a sprinkle of coconut milk and scallions on top.

Nutritional Value: Calories: 145, Fat: 7g, Carb: 20g, Protein: 2g, Fiber: 5g, Sugar: 10g, Sodium: 803mg

11.6 Cream of Cauliflower Soup

Prep Time: 15 mins. Cook Time: 1 hour
Ingredients:
- large head cauliflower, Half , cut into florets
- olive oil 1 tbsp. divided in two
- Half tsp. salt
- Half tsp. . black pepper, freshly ground, divided
- Half tsp. dried thyme
- one small yellow onion, cubes
- one clove garlic, chopped
- two cups slow-sodium vegetable stock
- Half tsp. liquid smoke
- Half tbsp. butter
- Half tbsp. fresh lime
- 1/eight tsp. . ground nutmeg

Procedure:
1. Preheat the oven to 420 degrees F. (215 degrees Celsius). Line a large, rimmed baking sheet with parchment paper or a silicone baking mat. Combine the cauliflower, ½ tbsp. olive oil, ¼ tsp. salt, ¼ tsp. pepper, and the thyme in a large mixing basin. Arrange the cauliflower in a single layer on the baking sheet that has been prepared. Preheat the oven to 250 degrees Fahrenheit. Preheat oven to 350°F and bake for 25 minutes, or until golden brown.
2. In a large stockpot, heat the last tablespoon of olive oil over medium heat. Turning occasionally, cook the onion over low heat for 5 minutes, or until it is lightly browned. Stir often for 30 seconds, or until the garlic is fragrant. When the cauliflower is thoroughly cooked, remove the pan from the heat and put it aside.
3. In a large saucepan, combine the roasted cauliflower, vegetable stock, and liquid smoke. Bring to a low boil, stirring regularly, over medium to high heat. Reduce the heat to a low simmer after the water has reached a boil. Cook for 20 minutes, stirring occasionally, to enable the flavours to mingle.
4. Utilize a blender or an immersion blender to purée the soup. To finish the soup, include the butter, lemon juice, and nutmeg.

Nutritional Value: Calories: 584, Fat: 20.4g, Carbs: 100.4g, Protein: 11.5g, Fiber: 14.6g, Sugar: 77.7g, Sodium: 1654mg.

11.7 Spring Pea Soup

Prep Time: 15 mins. Cook Time: 1 hr. Serves: 6 cups in 1 cup portions

Ingredients:

- 1 (16oz, 450g) bag freeze peas
- one little white onion, minced
- Half cup minced carrots
- 1 stalk celery with leaves, minced
- one clove-garlic, chopped
- three cups low-salt veggie stock
- Half tbsp. liquid smoke
- ¼ tsp. dry oregano
- quarter tsp. dry basil
- one/8 tsp. ground cumin
- 1 bay leaf
- 1 tsp. salt
- Quarter tsp. black pepper, freshly ground
- Crumbled turkey bacon (optional), to garnish

Procedure:

1. In a large stock pot, combine all of the ingredients. In a large saucepan over high heat, bring to a boil. Reduce to a low heat after it reaches a boil. Cook for 1 hour, stirring periodically, or until the vegetables are soft, covered. Remove the bay leaf and turn off the heat in the pan. Purée the soup with an immersion blender or gently pour into a blender and purée. Serve immediately with crumbled turkey bacon on top.

Nutritional Value: Calories: 67, Fat: 1g, Carb: 16g, Protein: 2g, Fiber: 4g, Sugar: 8g, Sodium: 545mg

11.8 Spring Vegetable and Chicken Puree*

Preparation Time: 5 minutes Cooking Time: 25 minutes Serves: 4

Ingredients:

- Extra-Virgin Olive Oil, 1 tablespoon
- Carrots, 2 small pieces, peeled and julienned
- Yellow Onion, ½ cup, diced
- Chicken Breast, 1 cup, cooked and shredded
- Chicken Bone Broth, 1 cup
- Salt, ¼ teaspoon

Procedure:

1. Heat the olive oil in a large saucepan over medium heat. Add the carrots and onions into the heated oil and sauté. Stir every 30 seconds or so to prevent the carrots and onions from sticking. The onion should be translucent while the carrots should be sufficiently softened. If the carrots are still hard, add a few tablespoons of water and cover the pan to help steam the carrot until it becomes soft.
2. Add the chicken, the chicken bone broth and the salt to the saucepan and bring the mixture to a boil. Lower the heat and allow to simmer for 7 to 9 minutes. This will allow the flavors to strengthen.
3. Switch off the heat and remove the pan from the burner to allow this to cool for at least 5 to 7 minutes. Once cooled, transfer to a food processor or a blender jar and puree for 2 minutes on low until smooth. Serve.

Nutritional Value: Calories: 357, Fat: 18g, Carb: 21g, Protein: 28g, Fiber: 4.9g, Sugar: 10.4g, Sodium: 3231mg

11.9 Cheesy Pommes Puree*

Preparation Time: 5 minutes Cooking Time: 15 minutes Serves: 5 in 1 cup portions

Ingredients:

- Russet Potatoes, 2 cups peeled and diced
- Part-Skim Cheddar Cheese, 1 cup, shredded
- Non-Fat, Plain Greek Yogurt, 1 cup

Procedure:

1. Prepare a pot and fill with 2 to 3 inches of water. Place a steamer basket in the pot. Add the potatoes into the basket and allow to steam, covered, for about

15 minutes or until softened. Remove from the steam.

2. Add the potatoes, cheese and yogurt into a blender jar or a food processor bowl and blend on low for about two minutes or until well incorporated and smooth. Serve warm.

Nutritional Value: Calories: 526, Fat: 7.9g, Carb: 73.2g, Protein: 52.5g, Fiber: 8g, Sugar: 14.1g, Sodium: 752mg

11.10 Pizza Puree*

Preparation Time: 5 minutes Cooking Time: 5 minutes Serves: 4 in 1 cup portions

Ingredients:

- Almond Milk, ½ cup, unsweetened
- Cornstarch, 1 tablespoon
- Part-Skim Mozzarella Cheese, 1 cup, shredded
- Canned, Diced Tomatoes, 1 cup, drained
- Salt, 1/8 teaspoon

Procedure:

1. Heat the almond milk in a medium saucepan over a medium flame. Rapidly whisk in the cornstarch and bring the mixture to a boil.
2. Reduce the heat to low and add the shredded Mozzarella, a tablespoon at a time, taking care to whisk continuously to ensure that the mixture becomes smooth.
3. Once the cheese has been thoroughly integrated with the milk. Remove the pan from the heat and allow to cool slightly.
4. Add the canned tomatoes and salt into a blender jar and blend on low for 20-seconds until smooth. Combine the cheese sauce with the pureed tomatoes in a separate bowl and stir to combine. Serve.

Nutritional Value: Calories: 386, Fat: 19.1g, Carb: 22.8g, Protein: 28.9g, Fiber: 1.6g, Sugar: 4.3g, Sodium: 1077mg

11.11 Puree of Butternut*

Preparation Time: 5 minutes Cooking Time: 15 minutes Serves: 5

Ingredients:

- Garlic Powder, ½ teaspoon
- Butternut Squash, 2 cups, diced
- Parmesan Cheese, ½ cup, shredded
- Non-Fat, Plain Greek Yogurt, 1 cup
- Sage Leaves, ¼ teaspoon, dried
- Salt, ¼ teaspoon

Procedure:

1. Fill the bottom of a medium saucepan with 2-3 inches of water and add a steamer basket. Add the diced butternut squash into the steamer basket and allow the water to boil. Steam the squash, covered, for 15 minutes or until softened. Remove from the heat.
2. Add the steamed squash and the remainder of the ingredients into the bowl of a food processor or a blender jar and blend or puree on low for about 2 minutes or until it reaches a smooth consistency. Store what you do not eat in an airtight container and keep refrigerated for up to 5 days.

Nutritional Value: Calories: 498, Fat: 11.3g, Carb: 55.5g, Protein: 46.1g, Fiber: 5.9g, Sugar: 24.5g, Sodium: 1451mg

12 BLENDED SMOOTHIES

12.1 High-Protein Fruit Smoothie

Prep Time: 5 mins.
Ingredients:
- Raspberry Yogurt protein powder, one scoop
- 3 strawberries or quarter cup blueberries
- 1-inch chunk banana
- half cup sugar-free vanilla yogurt
- Ice(cubes)

Procedure:
1. Add all contents in a mixing jar and mix till homogeneous.

Nutritional Value: Calories: 451, Fat: 3.8g, Carbs: 73.4g, Protein: 36.2g, Fiber: 13g, Sugar: 41.7g, Sodium: 494mg

12.2 Chocolate Protein Smoothie

Prep Time: 5 mins. Serves 1
Ingredients:
- one scoop ground chocolate protein
- one scoop ground vanilla protein mixed with 1/4 to Half tsp.
- half cup water
- One cup milk
- Ice(cubes)

Procedure:
1. Mix all contents together till homogeneous.

Nutritional Value: Calories: 245, Fat: 7.1g, Carb: 12.5g, Protein: 31g, Fiber: 1g, Sugar: 2.4g, Sodium: 648mg

12.3 Dreamsicle Smoothie

Prep Time: 5 mins.= Serves 1
Ingredients:
- one scoop ground Vanilla protein
- half tbsp sugarless orange syrup
- 1 cup water

Procedure:
1. Stir all ingredients together until smooth.

Nutritional Value: Calories: 271, Fat: 5g, Carbs: 23g, Protein: 30g, Fiber: 0g, Sugar: 16g, Sodium: 112mg

12.4 Root-Beer Float Protein Shake

Prep Time: 5 mins. Serves 1
Ingredients:
- vanilla protein powder, One scoop
- 1 tsp. vanilla extract
- 2 tbsps. sugar-free root beer syrup
- 2 cups water
- 6 ice cubes

Procedure:
1. Blend every ingredient collectively in a blending jar until creamy.

Nutritional Value: Calories 122, Total fat 3g, Carbs: 5.5g, Protein: 15g, Fiber: 0g, Sugar: 0.5g, Sodium: 391mg

12.5 Citrus Sunrise Shake

Prep Time: 5 mins. Serves 1
Ingredients:
- Juice from 1/2 of a lemon
- Juice from 1/2 of an orange
- 1 ¼ cups Ice cubes
- 3 Tbsp. Water
- 3 Tbsp. Splenda or other sweetener
- Orange wedges or lemon slices, optional

Procedure:
1. Add the juice from the orange and lemon halves to a 16-ounce shaker. Sweeten to your preference. Add ice cubes until the glass is two-thirds filled. Add water, seal the container, and shake. Use a big glass to serve it.

Nutritional Value: Calories 73, Total fat 1g, Carbs: 13.1g, Protein: 1.4g, Fiber: 0.6g, Sugar: 11.3g, Sodium: 26 mg

12.6 Banana Split Protein Shake

Prep Time: 5 mins. Serves 1
Ingredients:

- ice cubes - 3
- frozen strawberries - 4
- Pineapple - 1/4 c.
- a ripe banana
- vanilla or chocolate protein powder - 1 serving

Procedure:
1. Mix 1 scoop of protein powder in a food processor or blender. Blend the ice cubes, frozen strawberries, pineapple, and a ripe banana for 45 seconds until they are entirely smooth.

Nutritional Value: Calories 148, Total fat 4g, Carbs: 17g, Protein: 53g, Fiber: 5g, Sugar: 7g, Sodium: 193 mg

12.7 Superpacked Shake

Prep Time: 5 mins. Serves 1
Ingredients:

- Half cup fresh spinach
- Half kiwi fruit, peeled and cut into chunks
- ¼ medium cucumber, peeled
- ¼ small banana
- unsweetened almond milk or low-fat milk, 1/2 cup
- Half tbsp. ground flaxseed
- Half tsp. chia seeds
- 1 scoop (¼ cup) unflavored or vanilla protein powder
- 5 to 6 ice cubes

Procedure:
1. Add the ice cubes, protein powder, chia seeds, flaxseed, banana, milk, cucumber, spinach, and kiwi, to the blender container. Blend for 2 to 3 minutes on high until the shake is completely smooth. If the shake is too thick, blend in 2 to 4 tbsps. of water until the shake is thinned to your desired consistency.

Nutritional Value: Calories 148, Total fat 4g, Carbs: 17g, Protein: 13g, Fiber: 5g, Sugar: 7g, Sodium: 193 mg

12.8 Very Berry Protein Shake

Prep Time: 5 mins. Serves 1
Ingredients:

- low-fat milk or unsweetened soy milk, 1 cup
- mixed frozen berries, ¾ cup
- vanilla or plain protein powder 1 scoop (¼ cup)
- 5 ice cubes

Procedure:
1. Add all the ingredients in a blending jar, and blend until it reaches a creamy texture.

Nutritional Value: Calories: 126, Fat: 1g, Carbs: 14g, Protein: 15g, Fiber: 3g, Sugar: 10g, Sodium: 153mg

12.9 Spring Clean Green Protein Shake

Prep Time: 5 mins Makes: 1
Ingredients:

- unflavored protein powder, 1 scoop (¼ cup)
- Juice of Half lemon
- avocado, peeled, 1/8
- small handful fresh parsley, 1/2
- 1 loose handful spinach
- small Granny Smith apple, ¼
- medium banana, ¼
- water, ¾ cup

Procedure:
1. Combine all the ingredients into a blending jar jar, and blend until it reaches a smooth.

Nutritional Value: Calories: 133, Fat: 5g, Carbohydrates: 16g, Protein: 10g, Fiber: 4g, Sugar: 8g, Sodium: 38mg.

12.10 Piña Colada Protein Shake

Prep Time: 5 mins. Makes 1
Ingredients:
- Sugar substitute, for added sweetness (optional)
- 4 or 5 ice cubes
- vanilla protein powder, 1 scoop (¼ cup)
- coconut extract, Half tsp.
- frozen pineapple chunks, 1/2 cup
- low-fat cottage cheese, ¼ cup
- unsweetened coconut milk, ¾ cup

Procedure:
1. Add all the ingredients in a blending jar, and blend until it reaches a creamy texture

Nutritional Value: Calories: 195, Fat: 5g, Carbohydrates: 18g, Protein: 14g, Fiber: 1g, Sugar: 13g, Sodium: 250mg

13 EGGS

13.1 Scrambled Egg with Aged Cheddar

Prep Time: 10 mins. Cook Time: 10 mins. Serving Size: ½ cup to a cup of the scrambled eggs.
Ingredients:
- Nonstick cooking spray
- 4 ounces Extra-lean turkey sausage (nitrate-free)
- 1 large egg, beaten
- Fat-free milk, 1/8 cup
- Onion powder, ¼ tsp.
- Garlic powder, ¼ tsp.
- 1.5 ounces Extra-sharp Wisconsin Cheddar cheese, shredded

Procedure:
1. Coat a large pan with the cooking spray, or pour some Extra-virgin olive oil to coat the bottom and heat over a medium flame.
2. Use a wooden spoon to break up the turkey sausage into smaller pieces and brown it in a pan. Brown the meat until it is no longer pink in color and is cooked through.
3. In a medium bowl, combine eggs and milk. Add the onion and garlic powders.
4. Add the beaten egg to the skillet and cook for a few minutes. Using a rubber scraper or wooden spoon, stir the eggs for 5 minutes on medium-low heat until they are light and fluffy.
5. Serve the dish with the cheese on top and keep it warm.

Note: The cheese must be used sparingly in this dish due to its high fat content. However, to maximize the cheese flavor, be sure to use a cheddar that has been aged for a long time. The longer a cheese has been aged, the stronger its flavor will be, and the less amount you would have to use.

Nutritional Value: Calories: 169, Fat: 11g, Protein: 15g, Carbs: 2g, Fiber: 0g, Sugar: 1g, Sodium, 413mg

13.2 Scrambled Egg Burritos

Prep Time: 10 mins. Cook Time: 10 mins. Serves: 1
Ingredients:
- 12 eggs (2 eggs for a single serving)
- Low-fat milk, ¼ cup (reduce to 1/8 if for a single serving)
- Extra-virgin olive oil, 1 tsp.
- A quarter of an onion, chopped
- ½ red Capsicum, diced
- ½ green capsicum, diced
- (15-ounce) can black beans, half a can, drained and rinsed
- 1 (7- to 8-inch) whole-wheat tortilla (low-carb)
- ½ cup salsa, for serving

Procedure:
1. In a large bowl, mix the milk and eggs together. Set aside.

2. In a large pan, heat the olive oil over medium-high heat before adding the onion and peppers. Sauté for 2 to 3 minutes, or until tender. Stir in the beans to mix.
3. Finally, whisk the eggs. 5 minutes on low heat with a rubber spatula until the mixture is foamy and cooked to taste.
4. . To serve, split the eggs between the two tortillas. After folding in both

ends of the tortilla, tightly roll it to seal it.
5. Serve immediately, or store in a zip-top bag in the refrigerator for up to a week. Microwave each burrito for 60 to 90 seconds before eating. These will keep for up to a month in the freezer.

Nutritional Value: Calories: 250, Total fat 10g, Protein: 19g, Carbs: 28g, Fiber: 13g, Sugar: 1g, Sodium: 546mg

14 VEGETARIAN OPTIONS

14.1 Cauliflower Mash

Prep Time: 10 mins. Cook Time: 5 mins
Serving: 1 ½ cups
Ingredients
- 1 large head cauliflower or a smaller head for smaller servings
- ¼ cup water
- ⅓ cup low-fat buttermilk
- Minced garlic, 1 tbsp.
- Extra-virgin olive oil, 1 tbsp.

Procedure:
1. Break off small pieces of cauliflower from the head. Add the water to a big microwave-safe bowl. For about 5 minutes, cover the microwave and turn it on low heat. Alternatively, steam the cauliflower until tender. Drain the excess water from the bowl.
2. In a blender or food processor, puree the buttermilk, cauliflower, garlic, and olive oil until the cauliflower reaches a smooth consistency. If you want a finer product, sieve the cauliflower mash.
3. Serve warm.

Note: If you cannot find buttermilk in your grocery store, simply mix a tsp. of lemon juice with 1/3 cup of low-fat milk. Leave for 10 minutes until it looks like the milk has thickened.

Nutritional Value: Calories: 62, Fat: 2g, Carbs: 8g, Protein:3g, Fiber: 3g, Sugar: 3g, Sodium: 54mg

14.2 Oriental Hummus

Prep Time: 10 mins. Serving Size: 1 cup
Ingredients
- Extra-virgin olive oil, 1 tbsp.
- 1 garlic clove, peeled
- ground cumin, ¼ tsp.
- Tahini, 1/8 cup
- Freshly squeezed lemon juice, 2 tsps.(juice of 1 lemon)
- Salt
- Black Pepper, Freshly Ground
- Frozen edamame, thawed, rinsed, and drained, ¾ cup
- Cayenne Pepper (optional)
- 2 tbsps. water

Procedure:
1. Combine the lemon juice, cumin, garlic, olive oil, tahini, and edamame in a food processor. If you need to scrape down the sides, you can stop the process and do that.
2. Add salt and pepper to taste. Repeat until the mixture is uniform.
3. If you wish to thin the sauce, add 1 tablespoon. of water and grains Repeat until the appropriate consistency is achieved.
4. Serve with vegetable crudites.

Nutritional Value: Calories: 115, Fat: 9g, Carbohydrates: 6g, Protein: 4g, Fiber: 2g, Sugar: 1g, Sodium: 20mg

15 SPREADS AND DIPS

15.1 Autumn Pumpkin Spread

Prep and Cook Time: 45 mins Serves: 4
Ingredients

- pure pumpkin puree 15-ounces
- 2/3 cup Splenda Granular or other sweetener
- quarter cup maple syrup(no sugar)
- one tsp. lime juice
- quarter tsp. powder cinnamon
- one/eight tsp. powder cloves
- Sodium chloride's pinch

Procedure:

1. In an average heavy-duty skillet, mix the Splenda, cinnamon maple syrup, lemon juice, pumpkin, cloves, salt. Bring it to simmer, once boiling, reduce to a low heat. Cook, stirring often, for 45 min, or unless the sauce is dark and thick. Refrigerate in a jar and use as you would peanut butter.

Nutritional Value: Calories: 29 Fat: 0g, Carb: 7g, Protein: 1g, Fiber: 2 g, Sugar: 2 g, Sodium: 103 mg

15.2 Home-Made Shrimp Spread

Prep and Cook Time: 5 mins Serves: 1
Ingredients:

- Half pounds saute shrimp
- Quarter cup Hellmann's mayo(low fat)
- 1 scallion diced
- ¼ tsp. Old-Bay's Seasoning

Procedure:

1. In a blender, pulse the shrimp until crumbled but slightly lumpy. Place in a serving dish and serve. Next, insert the Old Bay seasoning, mayonnaise, and scallions into a food processor until the scallions are very finely chopped. In a mixing bowl, whisk together the shrimp and the flavorful mayo. If

needed, add a splash of water to get the right consistency.
Nutritional Value: Calories: 325 Fat: 6.3g, Carb: 4.8g, Protein: 58.2 g, Fiber: 0.2 g, Sugar: 0.1 g, Sodium: 731 mg

15.3 Warmed Spiced Applesauce

Prep and Cook Time: 40 mins. Serves, 1
Ingredients:

- 3 big apple
- 1 complete cinnamon stick
- Splenda granular or other sweetener

Procedure:

1. Quarter each apple, then peel and core each piece, sprinkle each piece with lemon juice to prevent oxidation, put prepped apples in a covered pot. In the apples, arrange the cinnamon sticks and add ¼ water cups. Heat to a simmer, then reduce to a gentle heat and simmer for thirty min, or until apples are indeed very tender. After removing the pan from the heat, dispose the cinnamon stalks. Crush the apples with a potato crusher or a hardwood spatula to get a smooth sauce. Add ½ cup Splenda and more to taste.

Nutritional Value: Calories 375, Fat: 1.3g, Carbs: 99.9g, Protein: 2.1g, Fiber: 19.8g, Sugar: 71.8g, Sodium: 7mg.

15.4 Baba Ganoush

Prep Time: 20 mins. Cook Time: 15 mins. Serves: 1 cup
Ingredients:

- 1 small aubergine, cut into ¼-in thicker circle
- One tsp. Sodium chloride
- One tsp. olive-oil
- One tbsp tahini
- one garlic clove

- one tbsp fresh squeezed lime
- Half tsp. Fresh black pepper powder
- One tsp. smoked paprika
- Half tsp. sumac
- quarter cup minced fresh parsley and basil

Procedure:

1. Heat ovens to 420 degrees F (215 degrees C). Layer a baking sheet with a parchment paper. Alternatively, you can grill the eggplant for a smokier flavor.
2. Inside a dish, mix the aubergine slices with 1 tsp. salt and olive oil until completely coated.
3. Line a work surface using dual layer of paper towels. Allow aubergine rounds

rest for 10 minutes on the paper towel. Additional paper towels can be used to blot off excess wetness.

4. Arrange the aubergines in a single layer on the prepared baking sheet. Cool after 14 minutes in the oven or grill. Once the aubergine has cooled, remove the skin.
5. In mixer, add the tahini, garlic, lemon juice, pepper, paprika, sumac, and remaining 1 tsp. salt and pulse until well combined. introduce the aubergine, and mix until creamy and homogeneous. Introduce parsley& basil and pulse until well combined.

Nutritional Value: Calories 96, Total Fat 6g, Total Carb 11g, Protein 3g, Fiber 5g, Sugar 5g, Sodium 589mg

16 STAGE 3 -SOFT FOOD PHASE

The soft food phase includes most types of poultry, egg preparations (especially poached or hard boiled), all types of seafood and soups. In this phase, you may also consume hot cereals such as oatmeal, unsweetened cereals that have been sufficiently softened with skimmed milk, baked potatoes and sweet potatoes, and pasta. Fruits and vegetables are acceptable here except for those with a high fiber content as your body has not sufficiently adjusted to these yet. When you do use fruits and vegetables, it is important that you peel and deseed all produce before you use them in any of these recipes.

17 SEAFOOD

17.1 Not Mom's Typical Tuna Noodle Casserole

Prep Time: 15 mins. Cook Time: 40 mins. Serves: 5

Ingredients:

- Nonstick cooking spray or olive oil
- Half medium red onion, chopped
- Half red capsicum, chopped
- ¾ cups diced tomato
- fresh green beans, Half cup
- Olive oil-based mayonnaise, 2 tbsps.
- Condensed cream of mushroom soup, Half (14.5-ounce) can
- low-fat milk, ¼ cup

- shredded Cheddar cheese, Half cup
- Black pepper, freshly ground, Half tsp.
- 1 (5-ounce) can brine-packed albacore tuna, drained

Procedure:

1. Heat the oven to 425°F.
2. Heat an olive-oil-coated big frying pan over medium-high heat. For 5 minutes, or until the veggies have softened, sauté the tomatoes, red capsicum, and onion. Turn off the heat and let the pan cool.
3. Trim off the stem ends and string of the green beans, and portion them into 3- to 4-inch pieces.
4. Fill a large saucepot ⅓ full with water, and set a steamer basket inside. Place

the pot over a high heat, and bring the water to a boil.

5. Add the green beans to the steamer basket, cover the pot, and reduce the heat to let the water simmer. Steam the green beans for 5 minutes. Immediately remove them from the heat (you can submerge them in an ice bath to stop the cooking), drain of excess water, and set aside.

6. Grease a 9-by-13-inch baking dish with the cooking spray, or olive oil.

7. Combine together the mayonnaise, condensed soup, milk, and cheese in a bowl. Season the mixture with the ground black pepper.

8. Mix sautéed veggies, green beans, and tuna. In a uniform layer, pour the mixture into the baking dish.

9. Bake for 30 minutes, or until the edges are browned. Serve immediately.

Nutritional Value: Calories: 147, Fat: 7g, Carbs: 6g, Protein: 15g,Fiber: 2g, Sugar: 2g, Sodium: 318mg

17.2 Salmon with an Herb-Crust

Prep Time: 10 mins. Cook Time: 20 mins. Serves: 1

Ingredients:

- 1 (2-ounce) salmon fillet
- 1 tsp. minced garlic
- Half tbsp. dried parsley
- ¼ tsp. dried thyme
- 1 tsp. freshly squeezed lemon
- 2 tbsps. grated Parmigiano-Reggiano cheese or other hard cheese.

Procedure:

1. The oven should be preheated at 425 degrees Fahrenheit. Use parchment paper or greaseproof paper to line a rimmed baking sheet. When using a gas oven, take particular care.

2. Arrange the salmon skin-side down on the baking sheet and tent with a second layer of parchment paper. Allow for ten minutes of baking.

3. For the herb crust, prepare the following: In a small dish, whisk together the garlic, parsley, thyme, lemon juice, and Parmigiano-Reggiano cheese.

4. Remove the salmon from the parchment paper wrapper. Cover the fillets with the herb-cheese crust gently using a pastry brush. Bake the salmon, uncovered, for about 5 minutes more. The salmon is done when the fish readily flakes with a fork.

Nutritional Value: Calories: 197, Fat: 10g, Carbs: 9g, Protein: 27g, Fiber: 1g, Sugar: 3g, Sodium: 222mg

17.3 Pesto Glazed Salmon

Prep Time: 5 mins. Cook Time: 20 mins. Serves: 1

Ingredients:

- 1 (6-ounce) salmon fillet
- Extra-virgin olive oil, Half tsp.
- Basil Pesto, 2 tbsps.

17.3.1 For the Pesto:
- fresh basil leaves, Half cup
- Parmigiano-Reggiano cheese, 1/8 cup
- Extra-virgin olive oil, 1 ¼ tbsps.
- Pine nuts (omit if you are allergic to nuts), 1 tbsp.
- Water, 1 tbsp.

To make the Pesto:

1. Add the basil, Parmigiano-Reggiano, olive oil, pine nuts, and water in a food processor. A blender would also work. If you have the patience, you can use a mortar and a pestle. Pulse until the mixture is smooth.

2. Serve immediately, or keep in an airtight container before serving. If pesto will be stored, add some olive oil to top it off to form a seal.

Salmon preparation:

1. Heat the oven to 275°F. Line a baking sheet with aluminum foil and lightly brush the foil with the olive oil.

2. Arrange the salmon fillet skin-side down on the baking sheet.
3. Spoon and spread a tbsp. of pesto on the fillet.
4. Roast the salmon for about 20 minutes, or just until opaque in the center. Watch carefully so you don't overcook the fish.

Nutritional Value: Calories: 182, Fat: 10g, Carbs: 1g , Protein: 20 g Fiber: 0 g , Sugar: 0g , Sodium: 90mg

17.4 Sweet and Tart Baked Halibut

Prep Time: 5 mins. Cook Time: 35 mins. Serves: 1-2

Ingredients:

- Extra-virgin olive oil, 1 Half tbsp.
- Half Vidalia onion or other sweet onion, chopped
- Half tbsp. minced garlic
- Half (10-ounce) container grape tomatoes
- 6 tbsps. dry white wine, divided
- 1 Half tbsps. capers
- ¾ pound thick-cut halibut fillet, deboned
- ¼ tsp. dried oregano
- Salt
- Black pepper, freshly ground

Procedure:

1. Heat the oven to 350°F.
2. Heat the olive oil in a Dutch oven or a large oven-safe skillet over a medium-high heat. Sauté the onion for approximately 3 to 5 minutes, or until caramelized and softened.
3. Add the garlic and sauté for 1 to 2 minutes, or until fragrant but not totally browned.
4. Cook for 5 minutes, or until the tomatoes begin to soften. Once the tomatoes begin to soften, gently crush them with a potato masher or fork to release their juices.
5. Stir in 3 tbsps. white wine to the pan. Cook for 2–3 minutes, or until the wine

has thickened somewhat. Include the capers.
6. Push the vegetables to the sides of the pan to create an opening in the center of the pan for the fish. Set the fish in the pan and season it with the oregano, salt, and pepper, then ladle the tomato mixture over the fish.
7. Pour in the remaining 3 tbsps. of wine.
8. Put the tray in the oven and bake for about 20 minutes, uncovered, or until the fish flakes easily with a fork. The fish can reach an internal temperature of 145°F on a thermometer. Serve warm.

Nutritional Value: Calories: 237, Fat: 10g, Carbs: 6g, Protein: 24g, Fiber: 1g, Sugar: 2g, Sodium: 166mg

17.5 Guiltless Corn-Crusted Cod

Prep Time: 15 mins. Cook Time: 10 mins. Serves: 2

Ingredients:

- Corn meal, 6 tbsps.
- Whole-wheat bread crumbs 6 tbsps.
- Lemon pepper seasoning, ¾ tsp.
- Onion powder, ¼ tsp.
- Garlic powder, ¼ tsp.
- Ground cayenne pepper, 1/8 tsp.
- 1 egg
- 2 (4-ounce) cod fillets
- Extra-virgin olive oil, ¾ tbsp.

Procedure:

1. Heat oven to 450°F.
2. In a large resealable bag, combine the cornmeal, bread crumbs, lemon pepper seasoning, onion powder, garlic powder, and cayenne pepper. Alternatively, combine all ingredients in a small dish prior to putting to the bag. Shake well to integrate.
3. In a small dish, lightly beat the eggs.
4. Gently insert the fish fillet into the bag, coating it with the cornmeal mixture. Following that, dip it in the egg and then a second time in the dry mixture.

Set aside one fillet on a platter and repeat with the other.

5. Preheat an oven-safe large skillet over medium heat. Allow time for the oil to heat up.
6. Add the fish to the skillet gently. Brown it on one side for 2 minutes, then carefully flip it over to brown the other side for an additional 2 minutes. Transfer the pan to the oven. Allow 6 minutes in the oven for the fish to split apart easily.

Nutritional Value: Calories: 297, Fat: 9g, Carbs: 28g, Protein: 27g, Fiber: 3g, Sugar: 0g, Sodium: 576mg

17.6 Mediterranean Style Baked Cod

Prep Time: 10 mins. Cook Time: 35 mins. Serves: 2

Ingredients:

- 1 tsps. Extra-virgin olive oil
- Half fennel bulb, sliced thinly
- 1/8 cup dry white wine or other white wine
- 3 tbsps. orange juice, freshly squeezed
- Half tsp. black pepper, freshly ground
- 2 (4-ounce) cod fillets
- 2 slices fresh orange (with rind)
- 1/8 cup Kalamata olives, pitted
- 1 bay leaves

Procedure:

1. Heat the oven to 400°F.
2. Add the olive oil to a large Dutch oven or oven-safe pan and heat over a medium burner. Add the fennel and simmer for about 8 to 10 minutes, stirring frequently, until it is softened and translucent.
3. Pour a glass of wine. Bring the mixture to a boil, then lower the heat and simmer for two minutes. Allow the mixture to boil for two minutes before serving.
4. After taking the pan out of the heat, put out the fish on top of it. Add a few slices of orange on the top of the fish

fillets. The fish fillets should be surrounded by olives and bay leaves.

5. Roast for 20 minutes, or until fish is opaque. The fish is done when it begins to flake easily with a fork or reaches an internal temperature of 145°F. Discard the bay leaves before you serve.

Nutritional Value: Calories: 186, Fat: 5g, Carbs: 8g, Protein: 21g, Fiber: 3g, Sugar: 4g, Sodium: 271mg

17.7 Mexican-Style Red Snapper

Prep Time: 20 mins. Cook Time: 10 mins. Serves: 3

Ingredients:

- 5 to 6 multicolored mini capsicums, stems trimmed, deseeded, and thinly sliced
- Half (10-ounce) container cherry tomatoes, halved
- Half cup fresh cilantro, roughly chopped
- 1 tbsp. capers
- Lime Juice from 1 lime
- Extra-virgin olive oil, 1 tbsp.
- Half jalapeño pepper, stem and seeds removed, finely diced (You can use hotter peppers if you would like)
- 2 (4-ounce) snapper fillets

Procedure:

1. Heat a grill to medium-low, or if you would like to do this indoors, Heat the oven to 425°F.
2. To make the salsa: Mix the mini capsicums, tomatoes, cilantro, capers, lime juice, olive oil, and jalapeño peppers. Set aside.
3. Lay out four 8 Half-by-11-inch sheets of aluminum foil on a clean work surface. One-quarter of the salsa mixture should be placed on top of a fish fillet before cooking. Wrap the fish in the foil and close the edges to keep out any air, moisture, or salsa that might leak out of the packet. Take another fillet and salsa mix, then repeat the process.

4. Close the grill's lid and place the foil packets on the grill, then turn the heat down to medium. Maintain a close eye on the temperature at all times. To avoid overcooking the fish, keep the grill temperature below 450°F. You want to cook the salmon until it is opaque, which takes 8 to 10 minutes. The heated air can scorch your fingertips if you open the foil packet.

5. When the fish begins to flake with a fork or reaches an internal temperature of 145 degrees Fahrenheit, it is done cooking.If using the oven, arrange the foil packets on a nonstick or lightly greased baking sheet and bake for 13 minutes, or until the fish begins to flake easily with a fork.

Nutritional Value: Calories: 161, Fat: 8g, Carbs: 7g, Protein: 15g, Fiber: 1g, Sugar: 4g, Sodium: 137mg

17.8 Summery Lemon Crab Cakes

Prep Time: 15 mins + 30 mins.. to chill. Cook Time: 30 mins. Serves: 2

Ingredients:

- 1 Half tbsps. whole-wheat bread crumbs
- 1 egg, lightly beaten
- ¼ tsp. Dijon mustard
- ¾ tbsp. olive oil-based mayonnaise
- Cayenne pepper, 1/8 tsp.
- Chopped fresh parsley, 1 tsp.
- Juice of ¼ lemon
- 1 (6-ounce) can lump crabmeat, drained and cartilage removed. If you can get fresh crabmeat, that would be good, be sure to check for stray bits of shell.
- Nonstick cooking spray or Extra-virgin olive oil.

Procedure:

1. Combine the bread crumbs, egg, mustard, mayonnaise, cayenne pepper, parsley, and lemon juice in a medium bowl until well-mixed.

2. Gently fold in the lump crabmeat taking care not to crush the meat.

3. Using a ¼-cup measuring cup, shape the mixture into 2 individual patties. Refrigerate the patties and let chill for 30 minutes.

4. Heat the oven to 500°F while the crab cakes rest in the refrigerator. Grease a baking sheet with the cooking spray or olive oil. Arrange the crab cakes on the baking sheet and bake on the center rack of the oven for 10 minutes or until they start to brown at the edges.

5. Serve immediately.

Nutritional Value: Calories: 148, Fat: 4g, Carbs: 5g, Protein: 21g, Fiber: 0g, Sugar: 1g, Sodium: 464mg

17.9 Shrimp Cocktail Greens

Prep Time: 10 mins. Cook Time: 5 mins. Serves: 2

Ingredients:

- Olive oil-based mayonnaise, 1/8 cup
- Half lemon, halved and seeded
- Half tbsp. whole black peppercorns
- Half tsp. dried thyme
- Half bay leaf
- Half pound unpeeled shrimp (31–35 count)
- 6 tbsps. cup Seafood Dressing
- Greek yogurt, 1 Half tbsp.
- 1 small head romaine lettuce, chopped
- ¼ seedless cucumber, chopped

17.9.1 For the Seafood Dressing:

- ¾ cup catsup (free of high-fructose corn syrup)
- 1 tbsp. grated horseradish
- Juice of Half lemon
- Half tbsp. Worcestershire sauce
- Half tsp. chili powder
- 1/8 tsp. black pepper, freshly ground

To make the dressing:

1. Combine the catsup, horseradish, lemon juice, Worcestershire sauce, chili powder, and pepper in a small bowl. Refrigerate and keep covered, for at

least 30 minutes or overnight for the flavors to mix well.

2. Serve with the desired seafood.

To assemble the salad

1. Fill a big pot with water and bring it to a boil. Add the lemon juice, black peppercorns, thyme, and bay leaf to the water. Bring the water to a boil in a large pot to make the poaching liquid.

2. Create an ice bath in a large bowl with ice and water as the water heats up. Set aside for later. This is to prevent overcooking of the shrimp.

3. Add the shrimp to the boiling water and cook them for 2 to 3 minutes, or until they are barely pink, but not rubbery. Drain the shrimp in a colander and immediately submerge in the ice bath to stop cooking.

4. Once cooled, peel the shrimp and remove the tails.

5. Combine the seafood sauce, yogurt, and mayonnaise in a large bowl. Mix well.

6. Stir the cooked shrimp into the dressing to evenly coat them.

7. Arrange the lettuce on plates. Toss the cucumber and top it with the dressed shrimp. Serve.

Nutritional Value: Calories: 163, Fat: 6g, Carbs: 4g, Protein: 17g, Fiber: 1g, Sugar: 4g, Sodium: 650mg

17.10 West Coast Seafood Stew

Prep Time: 15 mins. Cook Time: 45 mins. Serves: 4

Ingredients:

- 1 tsp. minced garlic
- Extra-virgin olive oil, Half tbsp.
- 1 leek, both white and green parts washed and cut into ⅛-inch slices,
- 1 celery stalk, cut into ¼-inch chunks
- Half green capsicum, diced
- 2 cups water, more may be needed
- ¾ cup dry white wine

- Half (10-ounce) container grape tomatoes
- Half large tomato, chopped into ¼-inch pieces
- Dried thyme, ¼ tsp.
- Dried basil, ¼ tsp.
- Half bay leaf
- Half tbsp. chopped fresh parsley
- Juice of ¼ lemon
- ¼ pound shrimp, deveined
- Half (6-ounce) can lump crabmeat, drained and cartilage removed
- ¼ pound scallops (freshwater or saltwater)
- Half tsp. black pepper, freshly ground

Procedure:

1. Over medium-high heat, place a large saucepan or Dutch oven. The leeks are briefly cooked in olive oil. Continue cooking the garlic for a few minutes, or until it begins to soften and release its flavour.

2. After 5 minutes, the green peppers and celery should be tender enough.

3. Combine all ingredients in a large saucepan and bring to a boil over high heat. Cover the stock and bring it to a boil. Let it simmer on the lowest setting for 25 minutes.

4. Remove the bay leaf and throw it away. Serve with a side of steamed rice or pasta. Other seafood, such as mussels and white fish, can now be added. Shrimp should be cooked for 5 to 10 minutes, or until they are no longer pink, while scallops should be cooked until they appear opaque. Sprinkle with black pepper to your liking.

5. Serve soup from a ladle into a bowl.

Nutritional Value: Calories: 171, Fat: 4g, Carbs: 5g, Protein: 21g, Fiber: 0g, Sugar: 1g, Sodium: 464mg

18 POULTRY

18.1 Creamy Chicken Cauliflower Potage

Prep Time: 10 mins. Cook Time: 40 mins.
Serves: 4

Ingredients:

- Half tsp. minced garlic
- Extra-virgin olive oil, Half tsp.
- Quarter of a yellow onion, diced
- Half of a carrot, diced
- Half of a celery stalk, diced
- 1 piece cooked chicken breast, cubed
- low-sodium chicken stock, 1 cup
- water, 1 cup
- black pepper, freshly ground, Half tsp.
- Half tsp. dried thyme
- 1 ¼ cups fresh cauliflower florets
- Half cup fresh spinach, chopped or other leafy, green vegetable
- 1 cup nonfat or 1% milk

Procedure:

1. Heat a large soup pot over a medium-high flame. Sauté the garlic in the olive oil for a minute until aromatic but not burnt or browned.
2. Slowly add the onion, carrot, and celery and sauté the vegetables until tender, 3 to 5 minutes.
3. Stir the chicken breast, stock, water, black pepper, thyme, and cauliflower. Bring to a simmer, reduce the heat to medium-low, and cook, uncovered, for 30 minutes, tasting each time.
4. Add the fresh spinach or chopped leafy, green vegetables and stir until wilted, about 5 minutes.
5. Stir in the milk and serve.

Nutritional Value: Calories: 164, Fat: 3g, Carbs: 5g, Protein: 25g, Fiber: 1g, Sugar: 4g, Sodium: 54mg

18.2 Barley with Chicken Vegetable Soup

Prep Time: 15 mins Cook Time: 50 mins.
Serves: 4

Ingredients:

- Extra-virgin olive oil, Half tbsp.
- Minced garlic, Half tsp.
- large onion, half then diced
- 1 chopped large carrot
- 1 chopped celery stalk
- diced tomatoes, Half (14.5-ounce) can
- pearl barley, ¼ cup
- 1 ¼ cups diced cooked chicken,
- low-sodium chicken stock, 2 cups
- water, 1 cup
- Dried thyme, ¼ tsp.
- Dried sage, ¼ tsp.
- Dried rosemary, 1/8 tsp.
- 1 bay leaves

Procedure:

1. Set a large soup pot over a medium-high heat. Heat the olive oil and sauté the garlic for 1 minute until aromatic, but not burnt.
2. Stir in the onion, carrots, and celery and sauté until tender, 3 to 5 minutes.
3. Pour the tomatoes, barley, chicken, stock, water, thyme, sage, rosemary, and bay leaves. Bring to a simmer, then reduce the heat to medium-low flame and cook, uncovered, for about 45 minutes. The soup is finished cooking once the pearl barley is tender.
4. Remove and discard bay leaves before serving.

Nutritional Value: Calories: 198, Fat: 3g, Carbs: 9g, Protein: 16g, Fiber: 2g, Sugar: 3g, Sodium: 528mg

18.3 Chili con Pavo

Prep Time: 10 mins. Cook Time: 8 hrs. Serves: 8. Ideal Serving: ½ cup

Ingredients

- Nonstick cooking spray
- ¼ pound Extra-lean ground turkey
- kidney beans, Half (14.5-ounce) can drained and rinsed
- diced tomatoes , ¼ (28-ounce) can with green chiles
- ¼ (8-ounce) can tomato puree
- small onion, finely chopped
- A quarter of a green capsicum, finely chopped
- 1 finely chopped celery stalk
- 1 tsp. minced garlic
- ¼ tsp. dried oregano
- Half tbsp. ground cumin
- ¾ tbsp. chili powder
- ¼ (8-ounce) can tomato juice

Procedure:

1. Combine all ingredients in a large saucepan and bring to a boil over high heat. Cover the stock and bring it to a boil. Let it simmer on the lowest setting for 25 minutes.
2. Prepare the base of the chili as the turkey meat browns. Add the beans, tomatoes, tomato puree, onion, capsicum, celery, garlic, oregano, cumin, chili powder, and tomato juice into the pot of the slow cooker. Stir in the cooked ground turkey and mix until well incorporated.
3. Cover the slow cooker and set on low to cook for 8 hours, watch the liquid when you can.
4. Garnish with Greek yogurt, shredded Cheddar cheese, and chopped scallions.

Nutritional Value: Calories: 140, Fat: 4g, Carbs: 12g, Protein: 14g, Fiber: 4g, Sugar: 4g, Sodium: 280mg

18.4 Chili con Pollo

Prep Time: 10 mins. Cook Time: 6 hours
Serves: 3 Ideal Serving: 1 cup

Ingredients:

- Chickpeas, Half (14.5-ounce) can drained and rinsed, divided
- Low-sodium chicken stock, Half cup divided
- boneless, skinless chicken breast, 1 piece
- Half large onion or 1 shallot, diced
- A jalapeño pepper or other chili, seeded, minced
- Ground cumin, ¼ tbsp.
- Ground coriander, ¾ tsps.
- Dried oregano, Half tsp.
- Chili powder, Half tsp.
- diced green chiles, Half (4-ounce) can
- Half cup water
- chopped cilantro 1/8 cup, for garnish (optional)

Procedure:

1. Prepare the bean puree first. In a blender or food processor, blend the beans with 1/8 cup of stock. Set aside.
2. Place the chicken breasts in a slow cooker about 4 to 6 quarts. Onion, jalapeo, cumin, coriander, oregano, chilli powder, and green chiles are layered on top.
3. Pour the remaining 1 cup of stock, water, remaining beans, and bean puree.
4. Cover the slow cooker, set the temperature to low, and set the timer for six hours. Transfer the chicken breast to a platter after five hours and thirty minutes and shred it with a fork. Return it to the slow cooker, and continue cooking on low for an additional 20 to 30 minutes before serving, allowing the chicken to absorb some of the stock.
5. Ladle into a bowl to serve and garnish with the cilantro.

Nutritional Value: Calories: 225, Fat: 3g, Carbs: 25g, Protein: 26g, Fiber: 7g, Sugar: 3g, Sodium: 661mg

18.5 Home-style Turkey Meatloaf

Prep Time: 10 mins. Cook Time: 1 hour
Serves: 2

Ingredients:
- rolled oats old-fashioned, ¼ cup
- Garlic, 1/2 clove
- ¼ medium onion, minced
- lean ground turkey, ¼ pound
- Worcestershire-sauce, 1 tbsp.
- ketchup, scattered, 1/8 cup and one tbsps.
- 1 large egg
- Half tbsp. Italian seasoning
- ¼ tbsp. of salt
- 1/8 tbsp. black pepper recently ground
- A cooking spray to prevent contents from sticking to surface

Procedure:
1. Turn on the oven and set the temperature to 350 degrees Fahrenheit
2. In a separate dish, combine Worcestershire sauce and two tbsp. tomato ketchup.
3. Gather all of the ingredients for the meatballs into a medium-sized mixing basin and combine thoroughly. When handling meat, be careful not to overwork it.
4. In either case, form it into a loaf and bake or pat it into a loaf pan oiled with butter. Add the sauce on top and mix well. If you have an instant-read thermometer that reads 165°F, you are done baking.
5. Remove the dish from the oven after 5 minutes and allow it to cool slightly before serving.

Nutritional Value: Calories: 258, Fat: 10g, Carbohydrates: 17g, Protein: 25g, Fiber: 2g, Sugar: 1g, Sodium: 665mg.

18.6 Asian-Chicken Lettuce Wraps

Prep Time: 5 mins. Cook Time: 20 mins.
Serves: 2

Ingredients:
- Half tbsp. coconut oil (or other vegetable oil if allergic)
- ¼ pound ground chicken
- 1 tbsp. soy sauce with a reduced salt content
- hoisin-sauce, 1/8 cup
- rice-wine vinegar,, 1 tbsp. lightly seared
- Half tbsp. spicy sauce (made with red chilli peppers and garlic) or any milder hot sauce
- 1 tbsp. of ginger freshly shredded
- One fresh chopped clove of garlic
- Finely chopped and strained 1/2 (eight-ounce) can water chestnut
- Butter lettuce leaves, for serving

Procedure:
1. Liquefy the coconut oil in a large saucepan over a moderate flame. While the chicken is cooking, break it up with a spatula as required.
2. Mix your hoisin sauce, vinegar, and sriracha in stand mixer in the same quantities as other ingredients. Cook for 5 minutes, swirling regularly, or until the majority of the fluid has been soaked. Sauté the veggies for 1 minute, or until soft, before adding the water chestnuts and ginger.
3. To make a single serving, pour 2 to 3 tsp. s of chicken mixture onto two lettuce leaves.

Nutritional Value: Calories: 285, Fat: 16g, Carbohydrates: 12g, Protein: 22g, Fiber: 1g, Sugar: 4g, Sodium: 802mg.

19 DESSERTS

19.1 Maple and Cinnamon Glazed Baked Peach

Prep Time: 5 mins. Cook Time: 30 mins. Serves: 2, half a peach per portion

Ingredients:

- 2 peach halves
- 1 Half tbsp. pure maple syrup
- Half tsp. ground cinnamon
- vanilla extract, Half tsp.
- A dash of salt

Procedure:

1. Put the oven to warm up to 350°F (175°C). Place the peaches cut-side facing up in a large baking dish or ramekin.
2. Whisk the maple syrup, vanilla, cinnamon, and salt in a small bowl until the salt has dissolved. Spoon the mixture over the peaches. Fill the centers and let run over the sides. Bake for 30 minutes or until the peaches can be pierced with a fork.

Nutritional Value: Calories: 102, Fat: 0g, Carb: 25g, Protein: 1g, Fiber: 3g, Sugar: 22g, Sodium: 147mg

19.2 Chocolate, Peanut Butter and Banana Ice Cream

Prep Time: 5 mins + 4 hrs. to freeze Serves: 2, in ½ cup portions

Ingredients:

- 4 ripe bananas
- 2 tbsp. unsweetened cocoa powder
- 2oz(55g) natural creamy peanut butter

Procedure:

1. Peel and slice the bananas. Arrange in a single layer on parchment-lined baking sheet or silicone mat, and freeze for 4 hours or overnight.

2. Combine all ingredients, and blend in a blender or food processor until smooth and creamy. If it becomes too soft, place the mixture inside a freezer for 10 to 30 minutes. Transfer to a lidded freezer-safe container for storage covered with cling film.

Nutritional Value: Calories: 196, Fat: 8g, Carb: 32g, Protein: 5g, Fiber: 5g, Sugar: 16g, Sodium: 62mg

19.3 Strawberry Cheesecake Sorbet

Prep Time: 21 mins Serves: 1

Ingredients:

- lemon juice, 1 tbsp.
- skim ricotta, ¾ cup
- frozen strawberries or other in-season fruit, 3 cups

Procedure:

1. Place the strawberries in a food processor, and then add the low-fat ricotta. After incorporating the lemon juice with the strawberries, puree until smooth.
2. Spread the strawberry mixture evenly in a container that is appropriate for the freezer. Place in the refrigerator. When ready to serve, portion out the mixture using a scoop.

Nutritional Value: Calories: 453, Fat: 21.2g, Carb: 51.3g, Protein: 21.2g, Fiber: 9.9g, Sugar: 36.2g, Sodium: 183mg

19.4 Chocolate Chia Pudding

Prep Time: 15 mins + 1 hr. to chill Serves: 2 in ½ cup portions

Ingredients:

- 1/2 cup unsweetened soy milk
- 3 drops liquid stevia
- quarter cup non sweet cocoa powder

- Quarter tsp. ground cinnamon
- quarter tsp. vanilla extract
- Half cup chia seeds
- Half cup fresh raspberries, for garnish

Procedure:

- In a small mixing basin, whisk together the soy milk, stevia, cocoa powder,

cinnamon, and vanilla until thoroughly blended. Add chia seeds and fully combine. Cover and freeze for at least one hour or overnight. Sprinkle with raspberries when ready to serve.

Nutritional Value: Calories 182, Fat: 9g, Carbs: 14g, Protein: 11g, Fiber: 14g, Sugars: 1g, Sodium: 36mg

20 STAGE 4 - REGULAR FOOD/STABILIZATION PHASE

In this phase, your body begins to accept the food that you would regularly eat, so you can move on from the purees and soft food items, though if you do want to eat them once more, go right ahead. There is nothing wrong with that. By this time, however, your stomach and your body begin to crave food with more substance, hence the regular food structure. There are some precautions that you must take however, in that the body requires a balanced diet that is free from empty calories. This means that you cannot indulge in sodas and potato chips among other items, though it

would be fine to have homemade potato chips if you wish to. It is important that you avoid high sugar and high fat food and go for snack options and food options that are packed full of vitamins and minerals. Now that your stomach has a lessened capacity for food, the nutritional value of the food content that goes into it is more crucial now as it has less food to obtain its nutrients from. You cannot eat a large amount of food to obtain your required nutritional intake for each vitamin and mineral so you would need to use vitamin supplements as well.

21 EGGS

21.1 Avocado Toast with Hard-Boiled Eggs

Prep Time: 10 mins. Cook Time: 8 mins.

Serving Size: 1 piece of toast.

Ingredients:

- 1 egg (You can add more if you want to prepare some ahead)
- 1 slice of sprouted whole-wheat bread
- Black pepper
- Half of a medium avocado
- 1 tsp. hot sauce

Procedure:

1. Prepare a pot of water large enough to boil four eggs, and allow to boil over a high heat.

2. Gently add the eggs to the boiling water, and set a timer for 10 minutes for a hard-boiled egg. Alternately, you can add the eggs into the pot of water before you set it on the heat, but be sure to note the time that the water begins to boil, and wait 10 minutes until the eggs are fully cooked.
3. Submerge the eggs in an ice bath or run them under a stream of cold water to stop the cooking process when they are done.
4. Peel and cut the eggs into four pieces after they have cooled enough to handle.
5. Toast the bread.
6. While the bread toasts, mash the avocado with a fork in a small bowl and add in the hot sauce, until you reach your desired spice level.

7. Spread the avocado mixture over the toast, add four egg segments atop each piece of toast. Season with the pepper.

Note: You can prepare the boiled eggs ahead as a time-saver. Be sure to store them in an airtight container as they can readily absorb strong flavors. The avocado mash cannot be prepared ahead, as this is best prepared fresh. If you do have leftover avocados, simply squeeze some lemon juice over it and store in an air-tight container to prevent the avocado from darkening.

Nutritional Value: Calories: 559, Fat: 14g, Protein: 14g, Carbs: 3g, Fiber: 15.8g, Sugar: 3.1g, Sodium, 353mg

21.2 Baked Mozzarella and Onion Egg Muffins

Cook Time: 25 minutes

Serving Size: 4 muffins

Ingredients:

- Grated skim Mozzarella cheese, ¼ cup
- Chopped onion. ¼ cup
- Extra-virgin olive oil, ½ tsp.
- coconut flour (if you have a coconut allergy, you may use another whole-grain flour) - 3 tbsp.
- organic eggs - 8

Procedure:

1. Heat the oven to 400 degrees Fahrenheit. Spray four muffin cups with nonstick cooking spray (olive oil is preferable, or some other vegetable oil).
2. Crack the eggs into a bowl and mix them together.
3. Whisk the eggs with the coconut flour or the flour of your choice until the flour is totally dissolved. Set aside temporarily.
4. Pour enough olive oil into a skillet to coat the bottom and heat over medium-high heat.
5. When the oil is hot, add the chopped onion and sauté until translucent, then

remove from heat. Allow to cool for a few minutes after removing from heat.
6. Add the onion that has been sautéed to the egg mixture, then completely combine.
7. Fill the muffin tins with the egg mixture, then top with grated Mozzarella cheese.
8. The egg mixture should be fully set after baking the muffins for about 20 minutes.
9. Remove the egg muffins from the oven when they are done baking. After cooling for a few minutes, serve them.

Nutritional Value: Calories: 855, Fat: 52.6g, Protein: 63.5g, Carbs: 30.6g, Fiber: 5.9g, Sugar: 5.4g, Sodium, 694mg

21.3 Vegetable Egg Casserole

Casseroles are a great way to prepare food in case you're in a time crunch, as it allows you to prepare several portions in one go, and all you have to do is reheat the leftovers. For a single serving however, you can half the recipe to accommodate your dietary needs

Prep Time: 10 mins. Cook Time: 40 mins.

Serves: 12

Ingredients:

- Nonstick cooking spray
- 1 onion, diced
- ½ cup mushrooms, chopped
- 2 cups roughly chopped broccoli florets
- 12 eggs
- 2 tbsps. low-fat milk
- Dried oregano, ½ tsp.
- Dried basil, ½ tsp.
- Dried thyme, ¼ tsp.
- 1 cup chopped or shredded cooked poultry breast, such as leftover turkey or chicken,
- canned chicken breast, or turkey lunch meat (nitrate-free)
- Extra-virgin olive oil, 2 tsps.
- Swiss cheese, 1 cup shredded

- Parmigiano-Reggiano cheese, ¼ cup shredded

Procedure:

1. Heat the oven to 350°F. Spray a 9-by-13-inch baking dish with the cooking spray.
2. In a large pan over medium heat, add the olive oil. When the oil is hot, add the onion and sauté for 1 to 2 minutes, or until tender. Add the mushrooms and cook for an additional 2 to 3 minutes, or until tender.
3. To prepare the broccoli, place the florets in a steamer or microwave-safe dish and add 2 tbsp of water. It should take around 4 minutes to cook in a microwave or steamer. Set aside any liquid that has been drained.
4. In a large bowl, whisk together the eggs, milk, oregano, basil, and thyme. Add the cooked vegetables, poultry, and Swiss cheese to the egg mixture and stir to combine.
5. Pour the mixture into the baking dish and sprinkle the Parmigiano-Reggiano cheese over the top.
6. Bake for 35 to 40 minutes, or until lightly browned. Let the casserole rest for 5 minutes before serving.
7. Store leftovers in the refrigerator for up to 1 week. Reheat before eating.

Nutritional Value: Calories: 147, Fat: 10g, Protein: 12g, Carbs: 2g, Fiber: 1g, Sugar: 0g, Sodium: 193mg

21.4 Savory Egg Muffins

This basic recipe can yield several portions that make it a handy tool, especially if you need breakfast on the go. Just prepare the night before, and pop it into the oven to reheat.

Cook Time: 20-25 mins.

Serves: 12

Ingredients:

- 6 large eggs
- Pre-cooked turkey bacon, 12 slices divided into 1/3 portions.
- Low fat cheese (Swiss or Jack would be good, preferably a good melting cheese) ¾ cup shredded, ¼ of the cheese should be set aside for topping the egg muffin.
- ¼ cup diced red pepper (optional)
- 1 tsp. diced green onion (optional)
- 1% milk, ½ cup
- Salt, ¼ tsp.
- Pepper, ¼ tsp.
- Italian seasoning, ¼ tsp.

Procedure:

1. Layer the muffin pan with cooking spray or a thin coat of oil.
2. Open the oven and set it to 350°F.
3. In each muffin tray, place three bacon slices on the bottom.
4. In a second bowl, mix together the rest of the ingredients, except for 14 cups of the shredded cheese, until thoroughly combined.
5. Take care not to overfill each muffin cup with the egg mixture.
6. Top muffins with an additional 14 cups of cheese.
7. Bake for about 20-25 minutes, or until the eggs have risen to the surface.

Nutritional Value: Calories: 147, Fat: 10g, Protein: 12g, Carbs: 2g, Fiber: 1g, Sugar: 0g, Sodium: 193mg

22 VEGETARIAN OPTIONS

22.1 Cauliflower Couscous

Prep Time: 5 mins. Cook Time: 5 mins. Servings: 11/2 cups.

Ingredients:

- cauliflower head, 1
- Extra-virgin olive oil, 1 tsp.

Procedure:

1. The first step in preparing cauliflower is to remove the cauliflower's stems and leaves. Slice it into four big chunks.
2. Make cauliflower rice by grinding the cauliflower in a food processor until it resembles rice. Cauliflower can be shredded with a box grater.
3. Pat the riced cauliflower dry with a paper towel before storing it in a container.
4. Coat the bottom of a small pot with olive oil. When the oil is hot, add the cauliflower. When the vegetables are fork-tender, cook for another 5 to 6 minutes. Cauliflower rice can also be steamed. Before serving, remove any excess moisture.

Nutritional Value: Calories: 12, Fat: 0g, Carbs: 2g, Protein: 1g, Fiber: 1g, Sugar: 1g, Sodium: 5mg

22.2 Fried Rice

Prep Time, 15 mins. Cook Time: 15 mins. Serving: 2

Ingredients:

- cauliflower rice (see recipe immediately before this), 1 cup
- 1 large egg, beaten
- sesame oil, ½ tsp. plus 1 tbsp.
- 1/2 cup frozen mixed vegetables or diced carrots, corn and peas.
- 1 garlic clove, minced
- 1 tbsp. low-sodium soy sauce
- 1 scallion, diced

Procedure

1. In a large saucepan, heat the sesame oil over medium heat. Scramble the egg until it is done. Set aside.
2. In the same skillet, heat the remaining tablespoon of butter. of oil. Add the eggs, cauliflower rice, veggies, garlic, soy sauce, scallions, and soy sauce. Cook, stirring regularly, for four minutes, or until the rice is well-combined and the cauliflower rice has softened. If the cauliflower is overcooked, it will get soggy.

Nutritional Value: Calories: 121, Fat: 7g, Carbohydrates: 9g, Protein: 6g, , Fiber: 3g, Sugar: 3g, Sodium: 357mg.

22.3 Roasted Vegetables

Prep Time: 5 mins. Cook Time: 30 mins. Serves: 3

Ingredients:

- Extra-virgin olive oil, 1 tbsp. or enough to drizzle over the vegetables
- Grape tomatoes, ½ pint
- Small courgette, 1, sliced into rounds
- Small onion, 1, halved then sliced
- Medium-sized capsicum, 1 cut into strips
- Salt
- Black Pepper, freshly ground
- Garlic Powder (optional)
- Paprika (optional)

Procedure:

1. Heat the oven to 400°F.
2. To ensure consistent cooking, place the veggies in a single layer on 1 large baking sheet. Wrap with foil.
3. Either with a spoon or your hands, toss the vegetables in the olive oil until they are uniformly covered. Use salt and

pepper according to personal preference.

4. After 15 to 20 minutes of roasting, uncover and cook for an additional 5 minutes, or until tender and lightly browned. Prepare it hot.

Nutritional Value: Calories: 75, Fat: 5g, Carbohydrates: 8g, Protein: 0g, Fiber: 1g, Sugar: 4g, Sodium: 2mg.

22.4 Deconstructed Caprese Salad

Prep Time: 10 mins. Cook Time: 15 mins. Serves: 6

Ingredients:

- cherry tomatoes, 24
- mozzarella balls, 12
- fresh basil leaves, 12

Balsamic Glaze and Olive Oil Dressing

- Balsamic vinegar, ½ cup
- Extra-virgin olive oil, 2 tbsps.
- 1 minced garlic clove,
- 1 tsp. Italian seasoning

Procedure:

1. Prepare twelve toothpicks or little skewers. Start each skewer with 1 cherry tomato, 1 mozzarella ball, 1 basil leaf, and finish with another tomato. Place on a serving platter if it will be served immediately, or keep refrigerated in a sealed container.
2. In a small saucepan, boil the balsamic vinegar.Simmer for 15 minutes until it reaches the consistency of syrup. Set aside to cool.
3. In a small bowl, combine the olive oil, garlic, Italian spice, and cooled vinegar.
4. Drizzle the skewers with the olive oil and balsamic glaze. Serve immediately as appetisers or preserve for later consumption.

Nutritional Value: Calories: 39, Fat: 3g, Protein: 1g, Carbohydrates: 3g, Fiber: 0g, Sugar: 0g, Sodium: 11mg.

22.5 Chopped Greek Salad

Prep Time: 15 mins. Serves: 3

Ingredients:

- 1 medium English cucumber, chopped (1 cup)
- ½ cup halved cherry tomatoes
- ½ red capsicum, seeded and diced
- ¼ red onion, diced
- Pitted Kalamata olives, ¼ cup, roughly chopped
- Crumbled feta cheese, ½ cup
- ¼ cup balsamic dressing

Procedure:

1. Toss all the ingredients together into a large bowl with the dressing and serve.

Nutritional Value: Calories: 173, Fat: 13g, Carbohydrates: 10g, Protein: 4g, Fiber: 1g, Sugar: 4g, Sodium: 883mg

22.6 Asian Slaw

Prep Time: 10 mins. Serves: 2

Ingredients:

- ½ (14-ounce) package coleslaw
- ½ red capsicum, thinly sliced
- ½ large carrot, grated
- 1/8 cup diced scallions
- Peanut Dressing, plus more if desired, ⅓ cup
- chopped peanuts, 1/8 cup
- chopped fresh cilantro, 1/8 cup

For the Peanut Dressing:

- 1/8 cup powdered peanut butter
- 1 tbsp. water
- 1 tbsp. rice vinegar
- 1 tbsp. low-sodium soy sauce
- ½ tsp. sesame oil
- ½ tsp. fresh ginger, minced
- ¼ tsp. sriracha (optional)
- ¼ tsp. fish sauce (optional)

Procedure:

To make the dressing:

1. Whisk all of the ingredients together in a medium-sized bowl.
2. Refrigerate in a container that is airtight. Maintains its freshness for one week.

To Assemble the Salad:

1. Combine all the salad ingredients in a large bowl with the dressing and mix thoroughly, adding more as needed.

Nutritional Value: Calories: 123, Fat: 6g, Carbohydrates: 16g, Protein: 6g, , Fiber: 6g, Sugar: 6g, Sodium: 198mg.

22.7 Vegetarian Chow Mein

Prep Time: 10 mins. Cook Time: 55 mins. Serves: 2

Ingredients:

- 1 tbsp, Extra-virgin olive oil
- Nonstick cooking spray
- 1 small (3- to 4-pound) spaghetti squash
- Low-sodium soy sauce, 1/8 cup
- 1 garlic clove, minced
- ½ tbsp. oyster sauce
- ½ inch piece of ginger peeled and minced
- ½ small white onion, diced
- 1 celery stalk, thinly sliced
- 1 cups shredded cabbage (or coleslaw mix)

Procedure:

1. The oven should be preheated to 350°F. Before baking, gently coat a baking sheet with cooking spray or olive oil.
2. Halve the squash and scrape out the seeds. Spread some cooking spray on the baking sheet and place both halves cut-side up. Assemble the spaghetti-like strands after baking for 30 to 45 minutes.
3. Wait until the food has cooled before removing it from the pan. You can

produce noodles by scraping the meat with a fork.
4. To make the dressing, combine the soy sauce, ginger, garlic, and oyster sauce in a small bowl.
5. Heat the oil in a big pan over medium heat. 3 minutes, stirring, until the onion and celery are softened. Stir in the cabbage and simmer for 2 minutes until cooked but not softened.
6. Add the spaghetti squash and dressing. Leave to cook for another two minutes, and serve immediately.

Nutritional Value: Calories: 252, Fat: 11g, Carbohydrates: 39g, Protein: 6g, Fiber: 9g, Sugar: 15g, Sodium: 950mg.

22.8 Vegetarian Lasagna Roll-Ups

Prep Time: 30 mins. Cook Time: 30 mins. Serves: 3

Ingredients

- part-skim shredded mozzarella, ½ cup
- marinara sauce, divided, ¾ cup
- Italian seasoning, 1 tsps.
- garlic, minced, 1 cloves
- Parmesan cheese, ¼ cup
- part-skim ricotta, ½ cup
- bag fresh spinach, ½ (10-ounce)
- 1 large egg
- Nonstick cooking spray
- Salt, ½ tsp.
- 1 large courgette, trimmed and sliced lengthwise into -inch-thick strips

Procedure:

1. Preheat the oven to 400 degrees Fahrenheit.
2. Salt the courgette slices and lay them flat on a baking sheet lined with paper towels. Let sit for 15 minutes.
3. In the meantime, heat a small pan coated with oil.
4. Remove the fire and cook the spinach until wilted.
5. Combine the Italian seasoning, egg, garlic, Parmesan and ricotta, in a medium bowl.

6. Pat the courgette dry. Take care to remove the excess salt and water.
7. Spread marinara sauce over the bottom of a 9-by-9-inch baking dish.
8. Roll each slice of courgette gently and lay seam-side down in the prepared baking dish, then top with a tsp. of ricotta mixture. Re-fill the remaining courgettes and repeat the process with the other ingredients.
9. Sprinkle the mozzarella cheese on top of the remaining marinara.
10. Bake for 26 to 29 minutes, or until the cheese begins to melt and the lasagna rolls are well warm.

Nutritional Value: Calories: 240, Fat: 13g, Carbohydrates: 16 g, Protein: 18 g, Fiber: 5g, Sugar: 7g, Sodium: 1019mg

22.9 Stuffed Summer Squash

Prep Time: 5 mins. Cook Time: 33 mins. Serves: 1

Ingredients

- Nonstick cooking spray
- ½ yellow summer squash
- ¼ cup Refried Black Beans (see recipe below) or canned fat-free refried pinto beans with taco seasoning added.
- ¼ cup cooked quinoa
- 1/8 cup shredded Colby Jack cheese or other melting cheese.
- 1 small tomato, diced
- 1 tbsp. sliced and pitted black olives, can be stuffed with capers.
- 1 chopped scallion for garnish.

For the Refried Black Beans:

- Extra-virgin olive oil, ½ tsp.
- Minced garlic, ½ tsp.
- ½ (15-ounce) can black beans, drained and rinsed
- Freshly squeezed lime juice, ½ tbsp.
- Smoked paprika, ½ tsp.
- Dried oregano, ¼ tsp.
- Cayenne pepper, 1/8 tsp.
- Ground cumin, ¼ tsp.

To make the Refried Beans:

1. In a small saucepan, heat the olive oil over medium heat and add the garlic. Add the beans and cook them for approximately 5 minutes, or until they are warm. Take the meal out of the oven or off the burner. Toss the zest of one lime and the herbs and spices together until well-combined.
2. Puree the beans using a blender or immersion blender, or mash the beans using a potato masher until they are the desired consistency.

To make the Stuffed Squash:

1. The oven should be preheated at 400 degrees Fahrenheit for step one. An 8-by-8-inch baking dish can be greased with cooking spray or a little layer of olive oil, depending on your preference.
2. Remove the summer squash's ends and throw them away. Scoop out the seeds by cutting lengthwise and then using a spoon. Prepare a baking dish by placing the cut-side-down half of the squash on the plate. Make a few holes in the squash with a fork to act as vents. To the dish, add 1 tbsp of water. Allow 3 minutes in the microwave or until the meat begins to soften. Throw away any extra water.
3. The squash should now be skin-side down when it has cooled sufficiently to handle.
4. Then add 1/8 cup of the quinoa and 1/8 cup of beans to the squash. Finally, add the cheese to the squash and serve. Bake it for 25 minutes with a foil cover.
5. The squash should be soft, and the cheese is bubbling when you remove the pan from the oven.
6. Before serving, arrange the vegetables and scallions on top of each squash. On top of the stuffing, you may add more protein sources like ground turkey.

Nutritional Value: Calories: 190, Fat: 8 g, Carbs: 21g, Protein: 9g, Fiber: 4g, Sugar: 3g, Sodium: 40mg

22.10 Mini Vegetarian Pizzas

Prep Time: 55 mins. Serves: 4

Ingredients:

- ½ Capsicum
- ½ Tomato
- ½ Aubergine
- Pesto sauce
- Extra-virgin olive oil, 1/ 8 cup
- Pinch of oregano
- 1 cloves of garlic
- Salt, 1/8 tsp.
- ½ sliced red onion
- Hummus
- Vegan Parmesan cheese or other Vegetarian Cheeses
- Whole Wheat Sandwich Thins
- Pepper Flakes to add Flavor

Procedure:

1. Heat the oven to 400°F.
2. Prepare the veggies by dicing them. Whisk together the pepper flakes, oregano, salt, pepper, and oil, in a separate bowl.
3. Arrange the veggies on a prepared baking sheet and roast until soft, approximately 32 to 44 minutes.
4. Toast the rolls, spread them with hummus, then top them with the vegetables and pesto sauce. Decorate with vegan cheese.

Nutritional Value: Calories: 462, Fat: 33g Carb: 39.3g Protein: 10.4g, Fiber: 12.4g, Sugar: 8.7g, Sodium: 697 mg

22.11 Easy Peasy Chickpea Salad

Prep Time: 7 mins. Serves: 1

Ingredients

- chopped raw vegetables (Use any vegetable you would like) ¾ cup
- Salt and Black Pepper, freshly ground to taste
- Chickpeas ¼ cup

- crumbled feta cheese ¼ cup
- Lemon juice, ¼ cup
- olive oil, ¼ cup
- dried oregano, ¼ tsp

Procedure:

1. Prepare your chopped vegetables, it can be a variety of seasonal vegetables to maximize nutrient use.
2. Rinse and drain the chickpeas.
3. Combine all the ingredients and chill in the refrigerator until serving.

Nutritional Value: Calories: 642, Fat: 59.4g, Carb: 24.6g Protein: 10.5mg, Fiber: 3g, Sugar: 7.3 g, Sodium: 794 mg

22.12 Tex-Mex Black Bean Cakes and Guacamole

Prep and Cook Time: 25 mins. Serves: 2

Ingredients:

- drained and rinsed black beans - 15 oz. or 1/2 can
- chipotle peppers in adobo sauce, set the sauce aside - 7 oz. or 1/2 can
- lime juice - ½ tbsp.
- diced avocado - ¼
- large egg - 1
- small tomato - ½
- ground cumin - ½ tsp.
- garlic cloves - 1
- chopped cilantro - ½ tbsps.
- whole wheat bread crumbs - ½ c.

Procedure:

1. Blend everything else in a food processor until smooth, approximately a minute, excluding the egg, lime juice and avocado.
2. Stir the egg into the mixture and pour everything into a large bowl. Make patties with the mixture.
3. Bake for 10 minutes until golden brown on a prepared, greased grill over medium heat.
4. Before serving, mash the avocado with a fork in a small dish with the lime juice. To up the ante, add chopped red pepper.

5. Serve with bean cakes topped to your liking.

Nutritional Value: Calories: 457, Fat: 16.2g, Carbs: 60.8 g, Protein: 20.6g, Fiber: 12.6g, Sugar: 7.4g, Sodium: 666mg

22.13 Southwestern Vegetarian Quesadillas with Yogurt Dip

Prep Time: 25 Mins. Serves: 3

Ingredients:

- shredded cheese - ½ c.
- ½ shredded carrot
- chopped cilantro - 1 tbsp.
- chopped capsicum - ¼
- black beans - ½ c.
- corn kernels - ¼ c.
- 2 corn tortillas

Procedure:

1. Prepare a pan by heating it gently. Place one tortilla on a baking sheet.
2. Place a second tortilla on top of the first and spread the vegetables out equally. Then add the beans, corn, and cheese.
3. Place the quesadilla in the pan and allow it to cook thoroughly. Ensure that the cheese has melted and that the tortilla has browned.
4. For a minute or so, cook the quesadilla on the other side.
5. Set aside the yogurt and cilantro mixture after thoroughly combining them. Serve the dip with the quesadillas, which should be sliced into four equal wedges.

Nutritional Value: Calories: 344, Fat: 8g, Carbs: 46g, Protein: 27g, Fiber: 12.4g, Sugars: 9.9g, Sodium: 541mg

22.14 Italian Stuffed Mushrooms

Prep Time: 30 mins. Serves: 2

Ingredients:

- easily to melt cheese - ¼ c.
- Roma tomato - 1
- 2 Portobello mushrooms - 2
- Pesto sauce - -2 tbsps.

Procedure:

1. Cut into little cubes the cheese and the Roma tomato
2. Heat the oven to 400 degrees F.
3. Spoon pesto in an even layer into the mushroom caps, then top with remaining ingredients.
4. After 15 mins of cooking, the cheese should have melted. Enjoy!

Nutritional Value: Calories: 112, Fat: 5.4g, Carbs: 7.5g, Protein: 10.5g, Fiber: 4.3g, Sugar: 6.7g, Sodium: 818mg

22.15 Vibrant Lemon Couscous

Prep Time: 25 mins. Serves: 2

Ingredients:

- fresh parsley - ¼ cup
- ¼ cucumber
- Couscous - 2.5 oz.
- vegetable stock - ½ cup
- Salt and olive oil (½ tbsp)
- lemon juice - ½ tbsp.
- tomato sauce - ½ tbsp.
- ½ onion
- ¼ carrot

Procedure:

1. Chop the parsley and the onion, slice the cucumber and the carrot
2. Boil the vegetable stock in a big pot on the stovetop. Slowly add the couscous. Keep covered for 10 minutes to allow the liquids to soak. Set couscous aside and fluff with a fork.
3. Olive oil and tomato sauce should be heated in a medium-sized pot. Heat the oil over medium-high heat in a large skillet and add the onion. Cool.
4. Mix all the ingredients except carrot and cucumber in a large bowl until well-coated. Toss until all of the vegetables are well-coated in the sauce.
5. Carrot and cucumber slices are an excellent final addition.

Nutritional Value: Calories: 720, Fat: 1.5 g, Carbs: 150.6g, Protein: 24.3g, Fiber: 12g, Sugar: 8.1g, Sodium: 592mg.

22.16 Summer Squash Lasagna

Prep Time: 1 h 50 mins. Serves: 3

Ingredients:

- grated parmesan cheese - 4 tsps.
- Ricotta - ½ c.
- roasted spaghetti squash - ½ c.
- marinara sauce - 1 c.
- shredded mozzarella cheese - 3 oz.
- red pepper flakes - 1/8 tsp.

Procedure:

1. The oven should be preheated to 375°F. Prepare a baking dish by smearing it half-way with marinara sauce.
2. The first layer of the lasagna should be squash, followed by the rest of the components.
3. Bake for about 17 minutes, or until the cheese has melted and the sides have browned. Cover with aluminum foil.
4. Continue baking the dish for a further 5 mins without covering it with foil. Serve right away.

Nutritional Value: Calories: 255, Fat: 15.9g, Carbs: 5.5g, Protein: 21.4g, Fiber: 7.6g, Sugar: 25.3g, Sodium: 1756mg

22.17 Southwestern Stuffed Sweet Potatoes

Prep Time: 35 mins. Serves: 2

Ingredients:

- salsa - ¼ c.
- ¼ diced red onion
- low-fat cheese blend - ¼ c.
- 2 medium sweet potatoes, baked
- Greek yogurt - ¼ c.
- olive oil - ½ tsp.
- ½ diced red pepper
- canned black beans - 2/3 c.
- chopped cilantro - 1/8 c.
- taco seasoning (see recipe under Vegetarian Enchilada Boats) - ½ tsp.

Procedure:

1. Mix the taco spice and yogurt. Put it in a cool zone.
2. Add the oil to a pan and bring it to a boil.
3. In a large saucepan over medium heat, combine all the ingredients except the sweet potatoes, cheese, and salsa, simmer for 8 minutes, occasionally stirring, until thoroughly heated.
4. Slightly puncture the middle of the potatoes and equally distribute the rest of the ingredients over them. Scoop off part of the sweet potato's flesh and mix with other ingredients if you like that option

Nutritional Value: Calories: 311, Fat: 8.3g, Carbs: 57g, Protein: 3.2g, Fiber: 19.1g, Sugar: 39.5g, Sodium: 1062mg

23 BEEF

23.1 Colonial Vegetable Beef Stew

Prep Time: 15 mins. Cook Time: 50 mins. Serves: 3

Ingredients:

- Extra-virgin olive oil, 2 tsps. divided
- beef sirloin steak - ½ pound
- minced garlic - 1 tsp.
- medium onion - ½
- ½ pound rutabaga, peeled, and cut into ½-inch cubes
- 1 medium carrot, peeled, and cut into ½-inch cubes
- 1 small tomato, diced
- Red pepper flakes - 1/8 tsp.
- Ground coriander - ¼ tsp.
- 1 tbsp. whole-wheat flour
- Smoked paprika - ½ tsp.
- ¼ cup red wine (it doesn't need to be vintage – cook with the kind of wine you would normally drink)
- 1 ½ cups low-sodium beef stock
- Fresh minced parsley, for garnish

Procedure:

1. Cut the beef into 1-inch cubes and chop the onion
2. In a Dutch oven or soup pot, heat 2 tbsps. olive oil.
3. Brown the beef cubes on all sides, rotating regularly, for about 5 minutes. Set aside in a bowl.
4. In the same saucepan, heat the remaining 2 tbsps. olive oil. Sauté garlic and onion for 1–2 minutes until soft.
5. Incorporate rutabagas, carrots and tomatoes with the paprika, coriander and red pepper flakes.
6. Cook the flour in the stew for 1 minute, stirring regularly. Stir in the red wine for a minute to blend it in.
7. Pour the stock and return the beef to the pot. Bring to a boil and then reduce the heat to low to simmer to thicken the sauce. Cook for 25-30 mins with the lid on. Garnish with the parsley.

Nutritional Value: Calories: 224, Fat: 10g, Carbs: 13g, Protein: 17g, Fiber: 3g, Sugars: 5g, Sodium: 139 mg

23.2 Pasta-Free Spaghetti and Beef Casserole

Prep Time: 10 mins. Cook Time: 75 mins. Serves: 4

Ingredients:

- Nonstick cooking spray or Extra-virgin olive oil
- 1 medium spaghetti squash
- ½ pound supreme lean ground beef
- ½ large onion, minced, or 1 small onion, minced.
- Half tsp. dried oregano
- 1 tsp. minced garlic
- Half can tomato sauce (8-ounce)
- Half can diced tomatoes (10-ounce)
- Half tsp. dried basil
- Half cup of a melting cheese like mozzarella
- ¼ cup shredded Parmigiano-Reggiano cheese or other sharp flavored cheese.

Procedure:

1. Preheat oven to 350F. Coat a baking sheet with cooking spray or olive oil.
2. The squash should be split half and placed on a baking sheet with the cut side down. Remove the seeds, pulp, and stems from the berries. Then cook the mixture in the oven for about 40 minutes.
3. While the squash bakes, spray or butter a big pan with cooking spray or olive oil. In a large skillet over medium-high heat,

brown the ground meat, onion, and garlic. Stir in the tomato sauce, diced tomatoes, basil, and oregano. Set aside the hot pan.

4. When the spaghetti squash has cooled, use a fork to delicately separate the meat from the outer skin. Place in a basin.

5. Place one-third of the meat-and-tomato mixture in the bottom of a 9-by-13-inch baking dish. Distribute half of the squash over the meat. 3rds of the meat and sauce over the squash Finish with the remaining squash and beef mixture. Add the two cheeses.

6. Bake for 30 minutes, covered with aluminium foil. Remove the cover and continue baking for another 10 minutes, or until the cheese starts to be brown. Serve hot.

Nutritional Value: Calories: 229, Fat: 10g, Carbs: 16g, Protein: 20g, Fiber: 3g, Sugar: 11g, Sodium: 511mg

23.3 Slow-Cooked Beef Sandwiches

Prep Time: 7 mins. Cook Time: 7 hours Serves: 3

Ingredients:

- dried thyme - 1/8 tsp.
- Black Pepper, freshly ground - 1/8 tsp.
- Water - ½ cup
- balsamic vinegar - ½ tbsp.
- garlic powder - 3/8 tsp.
- onion powder - 3/8 tsp.
- dried parsley - 1 tsp.
- dried oregano - 3/8 tsp.
- dried basil - ¼ tsp.
- boneless beef chuck roast, fat trimmed - ¾ pound
- ½ onion sliced
- ½ red capsicum, cut into strips
- 2 sprouted-grain hot dog buns or sandwich thins
- 1 jar pepperoncini (optional) - 16-ounce

Procedure:

1. In a small bowl, combine the water, balsamic vinegar, garlic powder, onion powder, parsley, oregano, thyme, basil, and black pepper.

2. Layer the beef in a single layer in the slow cooker and add the onion and capsicum.

3. Pour the mixture in Step 1 over the roast. Cover the slow cooker and cook on low for 7 hours. The meat should be tender and cooked through at the end. Cook longer if the meat is still tough.

4. Carefully transfer the roast to a cutting board and let rest.

5. Thinly slice the roast, save the leftovers for sandwich fixings.

6. Toast the buns or sandwich thins.

7. Layer each bun with the beef and top with the jus (liquid from the slow cooker), pepper, and onion. Serve with pepperoncini.

Nutritional Value: Calories: 351, Fat: 9g, Carbs: 30g, Protein: 31g, Fiber: 5g, Sugar: 5g, Sodium: 418mg

23.4 Home-Style Sloppy Joes

Prep Time: 10 mins. Cook Time: 30 mins. Serves: 4

Ingredients:

- Nonstick cooking spray or Extra-virgin olive oil
- ¾ pound supreme lean ground beef
- Chopped onion, ½ cup
- Chopped celery, ½ cup
- ½ (8-ounce) can tomato sauce
- catsup (free of high-fructose corn syrup), ¼ cup
- White vinegar, 1 tbsp.
- Worcestershire sauce, 1 tbsp.
- Dijon mustard, 1 tbsp.
- Brown sugar, ½ tbsp.

Procedure:

1. Grease a large pan with the cooking spray or olive oil, and heat it over medium. Add the beef and brown until it is no longer pink, about 10 minutes. Drain off any rendered beef fat and excess oil.
2. Add the onion and celery, and cook for 2 to 3 minutes until softened.

3. Stir in the tomato sauce, catsup, vinegar, Worcestershire sauce, mustard, and brown sugar and mix well. Bring the liquid to a simmer, and reduce the heat to low. Cook for 15 minutes, until the sauce thickens.
4. Spoon about ¾ cup of the sloppy Joe mixture onto each bowl. Serve warm.

Nutritional Value: Calories: 269, Fat: 5g, Carbs: 32g, Protein: 24g, Fiber: 6g, Sugar: 6g, Sodium: 656mg

24 POULTRY

24.1 Turkey Bacon Potato Soup

Prep Time: 10 mins. Cook Time: 30 mins. Serves: 3

Ingredients:

- 2 slices turkey bacon (nitrate-free)
- Extra-virgin olive oil, 1 tbsp.
- Whole-wheat flour, 1 Half tbsps.
- ¾ cups 1% milk
- ¾ cups vegetable or chicken stock
- 1 medium unpeeled russet potatoes, cut into 1-inch cubes
- ¼ cup low-fat plain Greek yogurt
- sharp Cheddar cheese, ¼ cup shredded
- chopped chives, 2 tbsps.

Procedure:

1. A big stockpot should be heated over a medium flame. Add the turkey bacon and fry until crisp on both sides, approximately 5 minutes, flipping once. Transfer to a plate lined with paper towels to absorb excess oil. After cooling, coarsely chop and set aside.
2. Heat the olive oil over medium heat in the same stockpot to create the roux. Add the flour and cook, stirring for 3 minutes until the flour is translucent and browned. Add the milk gradually while whisking continually until the mixture

begins to thicken. Slowly whisk in the stock.
3. Include potatoes. Reduce the heat to low and let the soup simmer for approximately 18 minutes, or until the potatoes are tender.Add the Greek yogurt and mix to combine well.
4. Garnish with the turkey bacon, cheese, chives, and some more of the Greek Yogurt.

Nutritional Value: Calories: 181, Fat: 9g, Carbs: 18g, Protein: 9g Fiber: 3g, Sugar: 1g, Sodium: 174mg

24.2 Grilled Buffalo-Chicken Wings

Prep Time: 15 mins. Cook Time: 20 mins. Serves: 9, Ideal Serving: 2-3 wings

Ingredients:

- Half pounds frozen chicken wings, skinless if you cannot tolerate the skin.
- Black pepper, freshly ground
- Half tsp. garlic powder
- Half cup buffalo wing sauce
- Half tsp. Extra-virgin olive oil

Procedure:

1. Heat the grill to 350°F. Season the wings with the black pepper and garlic powder, and rub to combine evenly.

2. Grill the wings for 15 minutes per side. Wings are cooked when browned and crispy. Mix the grilled wings in the buffalo wing sauce and olive oil before you serve.

Nutritional Value: : Calories: 82, Fat: 6g, Carbs: 1g, Protein: 7g, Fiber: 0g, Sugar: 0g, Sodium: 400mg

24.3 Country-Style Chicken Tenders with Peppercorn Ranch Dip

Prep Time: 10 mins. Cook Time: 20 mins. Serves: 3

Ingredients:

- Nonstick cooking spray
- 1 chicken tenderloin piece
- Whole-wheat pastry flour, 1 tbsp.
- Egg, lightly beaten
- whole-wheat bread crumbs, ¼ cup
- Grated Parmigiano-Reggiano cheese, Half tbsps.
- Dried parsley, Half tsps.
- Dried dill, ¼ tsp.
- Garlic powder, 1/8 tsp.
- Onion powder, 1/8 tsp.
- Dried basil, ¼ tsp.
- A pinch of black pepper, freshly ground

24.3.1 For the Peppercorn Ranch Dip:

- Plain Greek yogurt, 6 tbsps. low-fat
- Grated Parmigiano-Reggiano cheese, 6 tbsps.
- low-fat buttermilk, 1/8 cup (or 1 tsp. lemon juice mixed with 1/3 cup milk, let stand for 10 minutes)
- Juice of ¼ lemon
- Half tsps. black pepper, freshly ground
- Onion flakes, 1/8 tsp.
- Salt, 1/8 tsp.

To prepare the dipping sauce:

1. The onion flakes, lemon juice, yogurt, cheese, buttermilk, pepper, and salt should be pureed in a blender until entirely smooth.

To make the Chicken Tenders:

2. Preheat the oven to 425 degrees Fahrenheit. Apply cooking spray on a baking sheet.
3. Prepare the breading station: Set up three small dishes to coat the chicken. Add the flour in one, the beaten egg in the second, and in the last dish, combine the bread crumbs, Parmigiano-Reggiano cheese, parsley, dill, garlic powder, onion powder, basil, and black pepper until well-incorporated.
4. Bread one piece at a time, dip each piece into the flour. Shake off any excess flour, then dip the chicken into the egg. Finally, dredge the tenderloin in the bread crumbs and press to coat in the mixture. Arrange on the baking sheet.
5. Bake for about 20 minutes, or until crispy, brown and cooked through. Serve with the Peppercorn Ranch Dip.

Nutritional Value: Calories: 162, Fat: 2g, Carbs: 8g, Protein: 25g, Fiber: 1g, Sugar: 1g, Sodium: 239mg

24.4 Chicken Bell-Pepper Vegetable Nachos

Prep Time: 10 mins. Cook Time: 25 mins. Serves: 8

Ingredients:

- Nonstick cooking spray
- Half (1-pound) package mini capsicums, stemmed, seeded, and halved
- Extra-virgin olive oil, 1 tsp.
- Quarter of an onion or 1 shallot, finely diced.
- Half cup cooked shredded chicken breast
- 1 small tomato, diced

- Garlic powder, ¼ tsp.
- Ground cumin, ¼ tsp.
- Smoked paprika, ¼ tsp.
- shredded Colby Jack cheese or other low-fat cheese, ¼ cup
- sliced black olives, pitted, 1/8 cup
- 1 scallions, finely sliced, green parts only.
- 1 jalapeño pepper, seeded, thinly sliced or other chili pepper (garnish)

Procedure:

1. Heat the oven to 400°F. Line a baking tray with aluminum foil and coat the foil with the cooking spray or a light film of olive oil.
2. Arrange the capsicum halves in a single layer on the baking sheet with the cut-side up.
3. Heat the olive oil in a large pan over medium heat. Add the onion and sauté for 1 to 2 minutes, or until onions are soft. Add the shredded chicken, tomato, garlic powder, cumin, and paprika and cook for about 5 minutes, or until the tomato has softened and the chicken is thoroughly warmed.
4. Assemble the nachos by adding 1 heaping tbsp. of the chicken mixture into each mini capsicum half. Top each with the cheese, black olives, scallions, and jalapeño (if using).
5. Bake or broil for 15 minutes, or until cheese has melted and browned. Serve hot.

Nutritional Value: Calories: 189, Fat: 3g, Carbs: 9g, Protein: 29g, Fiber: 2g, Sugar: 2g, Sodium: 143mg

24.5 Buffalo Chicken Tortilla Wraps with Peppercorn Ranch Dip

Prep Time: 15 mins. Serves: 3

Ingredients:

- 1 Half cups cooked grilled, canned, or rotisserie chicken breast
- 1 cup chopped romaine lettuce
- Half tomato, diced
- 1 small red onion, finely sliced
- 6 tbsps. Buffalo wing sauce,
- 6 tbsps. Peppercorn Ranch Dip (see recipe under Country-Style Chicken Tenders)
- Chopped raw celery (optional)
- 2 small 100% whole-grain low-carb wraps

Procedure:

1. Combine the chicken, lettuce, tomato, onion, wing sauce, dressing, and celery (if using) in a large bowl.
2. Spoon about 1 cup of the mixture onto each wrap. Fold the wrap over the top of the salad, tuck in the sides, and then tightly roll the wrap closed. Use a toothpick to secure the wrap, if needed, and serve.

Nutritional Value: Calories: 200, Fat: 7g, Carbs: 14g, Protein: 28g, Fiber: 8g, Sugar: 2g, Sodium: 503 mg

24.6 Jamaican Jerked Chicken with Tropical Salsa

Prep Time: 15 mins + 30 mins to Marinate, Cook Time: 15 mins. Serves: 2

Ingredients:

- Extra-virgin olive oil, 2 tbsps.
- Juice of 1 lime
- Minced garlic, 1 tbsp.
- Ground ginger, 1 tsp.
- Dried thyme, Half tsp.
- Cinnamon, Half tsp.
- Ground allspice, Half tsp.
- Ground nutmeg, Half tsp.
- Cayenne pepper, ¼ tsp.
- Ground cloves, ¼ tsp.
- Black pepper, freshly ground, ¼ tsp.

- 1 4-oz boneless, skinless chicken breast
- 1 cup Mango Salsa

24.6.1   For the Mango Salsa:

- 1 large mango, peeled and diced
- fresh cilantro ¼ cup, finely chopped
- Lime juice from a whole lime
- ¼ jalapeño pepper, or other small chili pepper, deseeded, and diced
- ¼ large red onion or 1 small onion, finely diced (about ¼ cup)

To make the Salsa:

1. Combine the mango, cilantro, lime juice, jalapeño, and onion in a small bowl.
2. Enjoy immediately or store refrigerated in an airtight container for up to 3 days

To prepare the chicken:

1. In a gallon-size zip-top freezer bag, combine the olive oil, lime juice, garlic, ginger, thyme, cinnamon, allspice, nutmeg, cayenne, cloves, and black pepper. Tightly seal the bag and gently mix the marinade until well incorporated.
2. Add the chicken breasts to the marinade. Tightly seal the bag and shake to coat the chicken in the marinade or gently massage to ensure an even coating.
3. Refrigerate for at least 30 minutes or for best results: overnight.
4. Heat the grill to medium-high heat. Lay the marinated chicken on the grill and discard the marinade. Cook the chicken for about 6 minutes on each side depending on the thickness of the breasts or until the breasts are no longer pink in the middle and reach an internal temperature of 165°F. Alternatively, roast the chicken in a preheated 400°F oven for about 25 minutes, or until the juices run clear.
5. Slice the chicken once it has rested for five minutes. The Mango Salsa goes well with this.

Nutritional Value: Calories: 206, Fat: 9g, Carbs: 11g, Protein: 25g, Fiber: 1g, Sugar: 9g, Sodium: 111mg

24.7 Guilt-Free, Not-Fried Chicken Thighs

Prep Time: 10 mins. Cook Time: 35 mins. Serves: 2

Ingredients:

- Nonstick cooking spray or Extra-virgin olive oil
- Smoked paprika, ¼ tsp.
- Garlic powder, ¼ tsp.
- Black pepper, freshly ground, ¼ tsp.
- Cayenne pepper, ¼ tsp.
- Dried oregano, ¼ tsp.
- boneless, skinless chicken thigh, 1 (5-ounce)
- 1 large egg, beaten
- Half tbsp. water
- Half tsp. Dijon mustard
- 1 ¼ cups bran flakes or other whole-grain, unflavored cereal

Procedure:

1. Heat the oven to 400°F. Line a large rimmed baking tray with aluminum foil, and set it in the oven below a clean oven rack. Spray the clean rack with the cooking spray or olive oil.
2. In a large zip-top bag, prepare the rub: Combine the paprika, garlic powder, black pepper, cayenne pepper, and oregano until well mixed. Add the chicken thighs to the bag, seal the bag, and shake or massage gently to coat the thighs with the seasonings. Set aside.
3. In a small bowl, whisk together the egg, water, and mustard until well-combined.
4. Crush the bran flakes in another large Ziploc bag.
5. Bread the chicken: Dip the seasoned chicken thigh in the egg mixture, and then dredge them in the bag of crushed cereal. Shake to coat well.

6. Arrange the chicken thighs on the clean oven rack, making sure the baking sheet is directly under the chicken to catch any drippings.
7. Bake for 35 minutes, or until the thighs are crispy and reach an internal temperature of 165°F, and are no longer pink. Serve immediately.

Nutritional Value: Calories: 272, Fat: 8g, Carbs: 15g, Protein: 35g, Fiber: 3g, Sugar: 3g, Sodium: 279mg

24.8 Chinese Egg Roll Bowl

Prep Time: 10 mins. Cook Time: 20 mins. Serves: 3

Ingredients:

- Sesame oil, 1 tsp. divided
- Half tsp. garlic mince
- 1 small onion, finely diced
- ¼ pound Extra-lean ground chicken or turkey
- Low-sodium soy sauce, ¾ tbsp.
- low-sodium beef stock, ¼ cup
- Ground ginger, 1 tsp.
- ¼ tsp. black pepper, freshly ground
- green cabbage, 1 cup chopped or shredded into 1-inch ribbons
- ¾ cups shredded carrot
- ¼ cup fresh bean sprouts or 1 (14-ounce) can, drained, sprouts rinsed.
- 1 scallion, finely chopped, for garnish

Procedure:

1. Heat a large pan over a medium-high flame. Add Half tsp. of sesame oil and the garlic. Sauté for 1 minute. Add the onion and cook until softened, 1 to 2 minutes. Add the ground chicken or turkey. Cook until browned, breaking up the meat into smaller pieces with a wooden spoon or spatula, 7 to 9 minutes.
2. As the meat browns, mix together the remaining Half tsp. of the sesame oil, soy sauce, stock, ginger, and black pepper in a small bowl.

3. Once the chicken is cooked, add the sauce into the skillet. Add the cabbage, carrots, and bean sprouts. Stir to combine until well-coated with the sauce. Cover the pan and simmer until the cabbage is tender, 5 to 7 minutes.
4. Serve in a bowl and garnish with the scallions and additional soy sauce for flavor.

Nutritional Value: Calories: 133, Fat: 3g, Carbs: 7g, Protein: 19g, Fiber 2g, Sugars: 4g, Sodium: 356mg

24.9 Chicken Cordon Bleu

Prep Time: 15 mins. Cook Time: 30 mins. Serves: 3

Ingredients:

- Nonstick cooking spray or olive oil
- 1 3-oz piece of chicken breast, thinly sliced
- 1 slice lean deli ham (nitrate-free, about 1 oz.)
- 1 slice reduced-fat Swiss cheese, or Gruyere, halved
- 1 large egg, beaten
- Half tbsp. water
- 1/8 cup whole-wheat bread crumbs
- Half tbsp. grated Parmigiano-Reggiano cheese=

Procedure:

1. Preheat oven to 450°F. Apply cooking spray on a baking sheet.
2. Pound the chicken breasts to a thickness of 1/4 inch.
3. Put a ham and cheese slice on each chicken breast before baking. Carefully roll the chicken to secure the ham and cheese. Place it on the baking sheet with the seams facing out.
4. Prepare the breading station: Lightly whisk the eggs in a small bowl. In a second bowl, combine the bread crumbs and Parmigiano-Reggiano cheese.

5. Lightly brush each chicken roll using a pastry brush dipped with the egg wash and then sprinkle on the bread-crumb mixture.

6. Cook the chicken in the oven for 28 minutes, making sure it becomes lightly browned on top.

Nutritional Value: Calories: 174, Fat: 7g, Carbs: 3g, Protein: 24g, Fiber: 0g, Sugar: 0g, Sodium: 321mg

24.10 Turkey Meatballs with Vegetable Spaghetti

Prep Time: 15 mins. Cook Time: 20 minutes
Serves: 2

Ingredients:

- Nonstick cooking spray
- 1 large egg
- ¼ cup whole-wheat bread crumbs
- 6 tbsps. chopped onion
- Black pepper, freshly ground ¼ tsp.
- Extra-lean ground turkey, ¼ pound
- 1 medium courgette
- Extra-virgin olive oil, Half tsp.
- Half cup Herbed Marinara Sauce (a low-sugar jarred version may be used)

For the Marinara Sauce:

- Extra-virgin olive oil, Half tsp.
- 1 tsp. garlic, minced
- ¼ large yellow onion or one small onion, finely diced
- Half medium red capsicum, washed, seeded, and finely diced
- 5 to 6 fresh whole tomatoes, chopped, or Half (28-ounce) can crushed tomatoes
- Dried oregano, Half tsp.
- Red pepper flakes, 1/8 tsp.
- Dried basil, Half tsp.
- 1 bay leaf

To prepare the Marinara Sauce, follow these steps:

1. Over a medium burner, heat a saucepan. Sauté the garlic in the olive oil for 1-2 minutes, or until fragrant.
2. Add the red capsicum and onion. Cook, stirring regularly, for 2 minutes, or until softened. Combine the tomatoes, oregano, red pepper flakes, and basil in a mixing bowl. To blend, gently whisk everything together. Once the sauce is mixed correctly, add the bay leaves.
3. Cover, reduce the heat to medium-low, and let simmer for 30 minutes. Remove the lid and discard the bay leaves.
4. Use an immersion blender to puree the marinara to your desired consistency. Alternatively, transfer the sauce to a blender or food processor and pulse to achieve your desired consistency.

To assemble the pasta:

1. Heat the oven to 400°F. Grease the bottom of a shallow baking pan with the cooking spray or olive oil.
2. Combine the egg, bread crumbs, onion, and pepper in a large bowl. Add the ground turkey and with clean hands, mix well until the mixture is well integrated.
3. Shape the meat mixture into 2-inch balls and arrange in the baking pan in an even layer with enough space between each meatball.
4. Make the noodle soup: Cut the courgette's ends off. To make long, thin courgette strips, use a mandolin and a spiralizer.
5. Heat the olive oil in a medium pan over a medium flame. Add the courgette strips and sauté for about 5 minutes, or until tender. Transfer to a serving bowl.
6. Serve the meatballs over the noodles and top with the marinara sauce. 2 meatballs with ¼ cup of the noodles per serving.

Nutritional Value: Calories: 191, Fat: 5g, Carbs: 15g, Protein: 22g, Fiber: 3g, Sugar: 4g, Sodium: 205mg

24.11 Bean and Chicken Salad

Prep and Cook Time: 10 mins. Serves: 1 in 1 cup portions

Ingredients:

- one medium tomato (chopped)
- boiled rice (cooled) - ¼ cup
- black beans, cooked (drained) - ¼ cup
- low-fat cheddar cheese (shredded) - ¼ cup
- fresh parsley - ¼ tbsp.
- fat-free Italian salad dressing - 1/8 cup
- 3 leaves of lettuce
- lemon juice (fresh) - ¼ tbsp.
- cooked chicken (diced) - ¼ cup

Procedure:

1. In a large salad bowl, combine all ingredients except lime juice and Italian dressing.
2. Add the dressing and lime juice to the mixture. Add salt and pepper to taste and toss until all veggies are coated. Serve on a lettuce leaf.

Nutritional Value: Calories: 384, Fat: 6.6g, Carbs: 51.3g, Protein: 30.6g, Fiber: 9.2g, Sugar: 6.7g, Sodium: 219mg

24.12 Waldorf-Chicken Salad

Prep and Cook Time: 5 mins. Serves: 1 in 1 cup portions

Ingredients:

- 1 peeled and sliced poached chicken breast (See recipe to know more about how a chicken is poached)
- 1 tbsp. Mayo with low fat content
- Pecans, chopped (optional)
- 1 minced celery rib
- a peeled and sliced half apple
- a quarter cup grapes, half-sliced
- black pepper with salt
- Tarragon

Procedure:

1. In a mixing dish, mix the minced chicken and mayonnaise. Combine the chopped nuts, celery, apple, and grapes in a mixing bowl. sprinkle to taste.

Nutritional Value: Calories: 1201, Fat: 103.6g, Carbs: 39.9g, Protein: 43.4g, Fiber: 19.6g, Sugar: 19.6g, Sodium: 416mg

24.13 Basic Poached Chicken

Prep and Cook Time: 1 hr + 24 hrs cooling Serves: 4-5 in 1 cup portions

Ingredients:

- 1 frying chicken or 1 piece chicken
- 1 chopped carrot
- 1 chopped celery rib
- Cloves (whole)
- one small onion (white)
- Half tbsp. low-fat margarine
- Parsley Half tbsp.

Procedure:

1. To begin, place the chicken in a big pot in one layer. Include carrots and celery in your meal plan.Toss in the onion and all the garlic cloves to the pot when you're ready to prepare the poaching liquid. Toss in the parsley and margarine, then add sufficient water to submerge everything. After bringing the mixture to a boiling point, simmer for one hour, or until the chicken is done. A tilted cover and a sink full of ice water are all that is needed to keep the pot cool.
2. Two or three more times until the stock has cooled off. Refrigerate the chicken for at least 24 hours before cooking. break down the chicken.

Nutritional Value: Calories: 269, Fat: 7.74g, Carbs: 23.6g, Protein: 26.5g, Fiber: 7.1g, Sugar: 10.7g, Sodium: 290mg

24.14 Turkey Salad

Prep and Cook Time: 45 mins. Serves: 2

Ingredients:

- Turkey breast halves, skinless and boneless
- one/eight cup of walnut halves (coarsely diced)
- juicy yet firm half Bartlett pear
- olive oil Extra-virgin, half a spoonful
- ¾ tbsp. fresh lemon juice, to taste
- Half packaged salad greens

Procedure:

1. Prepare the oven to 350 degrees Fahrenheit (175 degrees C). Stack 2 layers of aluminium foil, each 24 inches long, on top of one another. Season the turkey breast with salt and black pepper before placing it in the centre of a piece of aluminium foil.
2. The remaining foil sheet should be placed over the turkey, and then the edges should be rolled together to seal the bird. For approximately 30 minutes or until the turkey is no more pinkish, bake the sealed foil bag on a baking pan.
3. Make the stuffing while the bird is roasting: In a small pan over moderate-low temperature, toast the walnuts for about five minutes, or until they begin to smell aromatic. To prepare a delightful dessert, grate the pears and combine them with the walnuts, oil, and lemon juice in a dish.
4. Let the turkey to lie for five min after removing it from the foil bag. Fill the dressing halfway with the drippings from the foil package. After combining the dressing, sprinkle salt and the pepper according to taste. Slice the turkey and arrange it on top of the lettuce on a serving tray. Before serving, drizzle the salad with the walnut and pear dressing.

Nutritional Value: Calories: 301, Fat: 24g, Carbs: 16.7g, Protein: 9.1g, Fiber: 4.1g, Sugar: 8.6g. Sodium: 278mg

24.15 Fall Chicken Salad

Prep and Cook Time: 30 mins. Serves: 2

Ingredients:

- marinated artichoke hearts (6 1/2 oz.) - 1/2 jar
- dried white wine - ½ tbsp.
- 1/4 garlic clove
- salt - 1/4 tsp
- crumbled oregano (dried) - ½ tsp.
- powdered pepper - 1/8 tsp
- seedless grapes - 1/3 cup
- sweet onion (slices) - 1/4 cup
- Capsicum, 1/2 red or yellow, cut into 1-inch squares
- cooked chicken breast, diced and without skin - 1 cup
- 1 big lettuce cup (not essential)

Procedure:

1. Remove the artichoke hearts from the jar and discard the liquid. In a small container or mug, combine the contents of the container with the wine, oregano, salt, and pepper. In an average mixing dish, combine antichoke hearts and entire grapes. The sweet onion should be cut in half and then in half again. Alternatively, marinate one chopped red onion for 20 minutes in a solution of equal parts water and sugar. Before adding the onion to the salad, make sure it's fully dry. To the grape, onion, and artichoke mixture, add capsicum cubes and garlic slivers. Mix with the seasoning thoroughly.
2. To bake, place the marinated mixture on a shallow baking sheet. Set the oven to 425 °F. fry for 15 to 18 min, or until grapes are plumped and veggies are brownish around the edges. After 7 min, give mixture a quick stir. Diced chicken or turkey may be added to the grapes and roasted veggies. Combine thoroughly. Heat up the salad and serve it in lettuce cups or salad bowls.

Nutritional Value: Calories: 580, Fat: 31.2g, Carbs: 18.2g, Protein: 43.2g, Fiber: 2.8g, Sugar: 32.7g, Sodium: 701mg.

24.16 Leftover Chicken Sandwiches

Prep and Cook Time: 15 mins. Serves: 2

Ingredients:

- ¼ cup leftover cooked chicken, diced
- one celery rib (diced)
- one coarsely diced shallot
- one apple, peeled and diced
- two tbsp. mayonnaise (reduced fat)
- two whole wheat bread slices
- one leaf of lettuce
- season with salt and pepper suiting your taste

Directions:

1. Mix the vegetable, chicken, and mayo together in an average-sized dish. Place a piece of bread on a plate and top with the salad. Serve with a side of lettuce and the other piece of bread.

Nutritional Value: Calories: 482, Fat: 23.7g, Carbs: 49.7g, Protein: 19.1g, Fiber: 10.4g, Sugar: 21.3g, Sodium: 709mg.

24.17 Chicken Pasta Salad

Prep and Cook Time: 45 mins + 24 hrs. chilling Serves: 2 in 1 cup portions

Ingredients:

- Half package pre-made seafood boil
- 1 skinless chicken breast
- Half yellow capsicum
- Half red capsicum
- Half green capsicum
- 1 small bunch of scallions
- 1/4 of a 5 1/2 oz. finely chopped black olive can, drained
- drained half of a 2 1/2 oz. can of thick slices green olives
- 1 garlic clove
- salted and peppered to taste
- half a box whole-grain three colour pasta(radiator, rotini or fusilli)

- one tbsp. of salt
- olive oil 1/4 cup
- one tbsp. of salt

Directions:

1. 1. Inside a big saucepan, bring the chicken breasts and the seafood boil mix to a boil. The chicken should be cooked through and no longer pink after around 30 minutes of cooking. take the chicken out of the oven and let it cool down completely. Make a separate pot of stock for the pasta and use it instead.

2. In a dish, cut the three capsicums into the desired shape, ideally chunky. The finest method to serve chicken is cubed. Green onion tops should be chopped off and placed in a small dish. To create the dressings, whisk together the olive oil, salt, and vinegar in a another bowl. In a large salad bowl, toss all of the components together, then add the olives and season with salt and vinegar to taste.

3. Now is the time to add the minced garlic. Prepare the spaghetti while the ingredients are marinating. Bring the chicken stock to a simmer with the water. Cook the pasta according to the package directions after you've added it. After the pasta is cooked to al dente, toss it with the other ingredients. Keep the meal in the fridge overnight for the best results.

Nutritional Value Calories: 986, Fat: 64.8g, Carb: 54.9g, Protein: 51.7g, Fiber: 6.8g, Sugar: 7.6g, Sodium: 1300mg

24.18 Chicken and Mushroom Stew

Prep and Cook Time: 6-8 hrs. Serves: 2

Ingredients:

- water - 1/2 can
- 98 percent low-fat or fat-free, cream of mushroom soup - 1/2 can

- One chicken breast - boneless and skinless
- salt (1/8 tsp.) and black pepper (1/4 tsp.)
- clean and sliced fresh medium sized white mushrooms - 1/4 pound
- Baby carrots - 1/2 cup
- One celery rib (chopped into tiny pieces)
- garlic powder - 1/4 tsp.

Directions:

1. In the slow cooker's pan, mix the soup and water together and set it to simmer.
2. After seasoned the chicken with salt and pepper, cut it into 2-inch slices. Combine all of the ingredients in a large slow cooker. On low for 7 hours, or until the chicken is done, cover the pot and cook.

Nutritional Value: Calories: 154, Fat: 2.9g, Carb: 6.7g, Protein: 24.8g, Fiber: 3g, Sugar: 2.9g, Sodium: 527mg

24.19 Chicken Cacciatore

Prep and Cook Time: 8 hours Serves: 2

Ingredients:

- 1 boneless, skinless, raw chicken breast, diced
- quarter pound of mushrooms(fresh)
- a half of a capsicum
- 1⁄2 of a capsicum
- a quarter of a 12-oz container of reduced-sodium chopped tomatoes
- a quarter of a reduced-sodium tomato paste can (6 oz.)
- a quarter of a 12-ounce can of reduced-sodium tomato sauce
- 1/eight tsp. oregano, dry
- Garlic powder, One/eighth tsp
- One/eighth tsp. salt and 1/8 tsp. black pepper

Procedure:

1. Combine ingredients in the slow cooker's pot. 8 hours on low heat with

the lid on, or until the chicken is done. Serve with whole wheat spaghetti.

Nutritional Value: Calories: 306, Fat: 4.6g, Carbs: 18.3g, Protein: 51g, Fiber: 5.1g, Sugar: 10g, Sodium: 658mg.

24.20 Chicken Jambalaya

Prep Time: 30 mins. Cook Time: 8-10 hrs. Serves: 4

Ingredients:

- 2 chicken thighs, boneless and skinless, chopped
- 1/2 green pepper, diced
- a big onion, cut in half
- 1 celery stalk, cut
- 1 garlic clove, crushed
- a half-can (14 oz.) of cut whole tomatoes
- 6 tbsps. paste of tomato
- a quarter can of beef stock (no fat content)
- a tbsp. of dry parsley
- 3/4 tsp. s of dry basil
- a tbsp. of dry parsley
- half tsp. salt
- four piece shrimp (peeled)
- one cup brown rice, cooked

Procedure:

1. In a rice cooker pot, combine all contents (excluding rice and shrimp). Cook for eight to ten hours on slow.
2. Add the cooked rice and raw shrimp in the final 15 min of cooking and complete cooking. Serve right away.

Nutritional Value: Calories: 1149, Fat: 39.6g, Carbs: 207.5g, Protein: 64.5g, Fiber: 23.7g, Sugar: 33.3g, Sodium: 804mg

24.21 Surf and Turf Gumbo

Prep and Cook Time: 1 hour Serves: 2

Ingredients:

- 1/8 cup whole wheat pastry flour

- a quarter tsp. of vegetable oil
- a quarter cup diced green capsicum
- a quarter cup diced green capsicum
- 1 diced garlic clove
- a quarter tsp. dry thyme
- 1 bay leaf
- 1 bay leaf
- a quarter can chopped tomatoes with juice (28 ounces)
- a quarter cup low-salt canned chicken or veggie stock
- a 1/2 tsp. of Creole or Cajun spices
- 1 6-ounce catfish fillet, sliced into 4 pieces
- 2 uncooked big shrimp, peeled and deveined

Directions:

1. Make the roux: In the bottom of a big, heavy saucepan, sprinkle the flour. Continue to stir flour over a low to medium heat until it gets nicely browned or richer (do not burn), approximately 15 min. In a mixing dish, place the browned flour.
2. Heat the oil in the same saucepan over moderate temperature. Cook until the onion and capsicum are soft, approximately 7 min. Stir in the garlic, thyme, and bay leaf for 1 min, or until fragrant. Mix with the crushed sausage and cook until brownish, approximately five min, splitting up bigger bits with a spoon, before adding the brown flour
3. the tomatoes, stock, and Creole spice to the pot with the preserved juices. Raise the temperature to high and bring the mixture to a simmer.
4. Turn down the heat to low, cover, and simmer for 20 min to allow the flavours to meld. Mix the mixture constantly. Add the catfish and shrimp to the saucepan and simmer it gently for 5 min, or until the seafood is opaque in the middle. Remove the bay leaf and season to taste with salt and pepper.

Nutritional Value: Calories: 783, Fat: 34g, Carbs: 16.2g, Protein: 96.6g, Fiber: 2.9g, Sugar: 0.9g, Sodium: 777mg

24.22 Turkey Rollatini

Prep and Cook Time: 20 mins + 2 hours chilling. Serves: 3 sausage patties

Ingredients:

- 8-ounce fat-free cream cheese half-package
- a quarter cup of roughly chopped carrot
- a quarter cup of roughly chopped courgette
- 1/2 tbsp. of dill weed, and a pinch of garlic powder
- to taste kosher salt and black pepper, freshly ground
- 1 deli-sliced smoked turkey breast

Procedure:

Combine the courgette, cream cheese, carrot, dill weed, garlic powder and cranberries in a shallow dish. Salt and pepper to your liking. The suggested amount of cream cheese mixture per turkey slice is 2 tsp. Clingfilm should be securely wrapped around the package.

Before serving, give yourself two hours to cool.

Nutritional Value: Calories: 82, Fat: 1g, Carbs: 7g, Protein: 10g, Fiber: 0g, Sugar: 6g, Sodium: 578 mg

24.23 Home-Made Turkey Sausage

Prep and Cook Time: 20 mins. Serves: 1

Ingredients:

- quarter lb. ground turkey meat (or pork as a substitute)
- salt, ¾ tsp.
- pepper, ¾ tsp.
- ground sage, quarter tsp.
- ground ginger, quarter tsp.

- red pepper flakes, quarter tsp.

Procedure:

1. In a large mixer, thoroughly incorporate and blend all of the ingredients. As desired, divide the mixture into 12 3-oz patties or links. Cover a nonstick pan with cooking spray and heat over a medium temperature to prepare the dish. Cook, turning occasionally to browned both sides, until the sausages are completely done.

Nutritional Value: Calories: 129, Fat: 7g, Carb: 0.3g, Protein: 15g, Fiber: 0.8g, Sugar: 0.1g, Sodium: 340mg,

24.24 Tandoori Chicken

Prep and Cook Time: 35 mins. Serves: 3

Ingredients:

- quarter cup plain yogurt
- quarter cup lime juice
- one chopped garlic clove
- one tbsp. paprika
- 1/2 tsp. yellowish curry powder
- quarter tsp. powdered ginger
- 1 chicken breast(skinless)
- 1 skewer

Procedure:

1. Prepare an oven to 400°F. Fresh red pepper flakes and yoghurt are blended until smooth with the remaining ingredients (excluding chicken) in a food processor or blender.
2. Thread chicken strips evenly onto chopsticks. In a small casserole dish, surround the chicken with 12 tbsps. of the yoghurt mix. Close the bag firmly and marinate for fifteen min in the fridge.
3. Brush a baking pan gently with olive oil, then arrange the chicken skewers on top. Preheat the oven to 350°F and put the chicken in the oven until it is completely cooked and no more pinkish in the centre.

Nutritional Value: Calories: 197, Fat: 7.2g, Carbs: 14.1g, Protein: 20.6g, Fiber: 3.3g, Sugar: 5.7g, Sodium: 108mg

24.25 Turkey Tostadas

Prep and Cook Time: 20 mins. Serves: 2

Ingredients:

- average tomato, 1/2
- sliced capsicum, 1/2
- dry oregano, 1/2 tsp.
- crushed chili pepper, 1/4 tsp.
- turkey breast, 1/4 lb.
- crushed garlic, 1/2 clove
- lime juice, 1/4 tbsp.
- olive-oil, 1 tbsp.
- quarter cup ripped cheddar cheese or any cheese
- 1 tostada bowl
- 1 tbsp. salsa

Procedure:

1. Combine oregano, chili powder, garlic, lemon juice, and 1/2 tbsp. of olive oil in a large mixing bowl. Make sure that the turkey flesh is well covered. Marinate for at least 30 minutes.
2. In a skillet over a moderate temperature, heat the remaining oil. Cook the capsicum for two minutes, stirring often, until it is tender. Cook for another 3 minutes, or until the turkey is cooked through. Remove the pan from the heat and mix in the tomato.
3. Spoon into a tostada dish the ingredients. Before serving, top with cheese and sauce.

Nutritional Value: Calories: 240, Fat: 15g, Carbs: 31.1g, Protein: 23g, Fiber: 5g, Sugar: 3.4g, Sodium: 403mg

24.26 Chicken Pesto Bake

Prep Time: 35 mins. Serves: 1, in half a breast.

Ingredients:

- 1 piece skinless chicken
- Half tsp. Basil
- Tomato's one slice
- 3 tbsps. ripped mozzarella cheese
- 1 tsp. Cheese (parmesan)

Procedure:

1. Chicken should be sliced in tiny pieces.
2. In advance heat the oven to 400 ° F. To avoid sticking, line a baking sheet with parchment paper or gently grease with olive oil or cooking sprays.
3. Place the chicken strips in a single layer on the cookie sheet that has been prepared. Brush the pesto all over the chicken pieces to cover them thoroughly.
4. Cook for 15 minutes, add tomatoes, mozzarella, and Parmigiano and cook until cheese has melted.

Nutritional Value: Calories: 205, Fat: 8.5g, Carbs: 2.5g, Protein: 30g, Fiber: 0.3g, Sugar: 0.7g, Sodium: 511mg

24.27 Chicken Tikka Masala

Prep Time: 15 mins. Cook Time: 30 mins Serves: 4 cups , in ½ cup portions with ½ cup Cauliflower Rice

Ingredients:

- ¾ cup plain nonfat Greek yogurt, divided
- 1 tbsp. garam masala, divided
- lemon juice, Half tbsp. freshly squeezed
- 1 tsp. fresh powdered black pepper
- fresh ginger, one slice peeled and grated
- Half yellow onion, minced
- 1 boneless, skinless chicken breast(diced)
- ¼ tbsp. butter
- one garlic clove, chopped
- Half jalapeno (optional), diced
- Half (15oz, 425g) can tomato sauce
- 6 tbsps. unsweetened coconut milk
- Half tsp. paprika
- Half tsp. salt
- Cauliflower Rice (to serve)

Procedure:

1. Combine 1 cup of yoghurt, 1/2 teaspoon of garam masala, lemon juice, black pepper, and ginger in a mixing bowl. Turn the chicken pieces to evenly coat them. For optimal results, refrigerate covered and cold for at least one hour or overnight.
2. The oil in a big, deep pan over medium to high heat. In a mixing dish, combine the chicken, onion, and marinade. Continue cooking for 5 minutes, or until the chicken is nearly done.
3. Reduce the heat to medium-low and stir in the butter, garlic, and jalapeño. Cook for about 1 minute, or until the garlic starts to smell aromatic. In a wide mixing dish, combine the tomato sauce, remaining 3/4 cup yoghurt, coconut milk, half tbsp. garam masala, paprika, and salt. Bring to a boil, then reduce heat to low. Twenty minutes on low heat are required. Stir often till the sauce thickens and the chicken is well cooked. Serves with cauliflower rice on the side.

Nutritional Value: Calories: 186, Fat: 8g, Carb: 11g, Protein: 19g, Fiber: 3g, Sugar: 5g, Sodium: 456mg

25 PORK

25.1 Spiced Pulled Pork

Prep Time: 10 mins. Cook Time: 6 hrs. Serves: 4, in ½ cup portions

Ingredients:

- Half (7.5-ounce) can chipotle peppers in adobo sauce
- Apple cider vinegar, ¾ tbsp.
- Powdered cumin, 1/2 tbsp.
- Dry oregano, 1/2 tbsp.
- Half of a Lime, juiced
- Half cup pork shoulder, trimmed of excess fat

Procedure:

1. In a mixing jar, puree chipotle pepper and adobo sauce, apple cider vinegar, cumin, oregano, and lime juice.
2. Set the pork shoulder in the pressure cooker and dump the blended sauce on it.
3. Cook on slow flame for 6 hrs, covered. When the pork shreds readily, it's done cooking. Shred the meat with two forks in the slow cooker. If there is any residual liquid, continue to boil the pork on low for another twenty minutes to soak it.

Nutritional Value: Calories: 260, Fat: 11g, Carbs: 5g, Protein: 20g, Fiber: 2g, Sugar: 2g, Sodium: 705mg

25.2 One-Pan Autumn Pork Chops

Prep Time: 10 mins. Cook Time: 30 mins. Serves: 2 pork chops

Ingredients:

- Extra-virgin olive oil, 1 tsp. divided
- Boneless center-cut thin pork chop
- 1 thinly sliced small apple

- Half , thinly sliced small red onion,
- low-sodium chicken stock, Half cup
- Half tsp. Dijon mustard
- Half tsp. dried sage
- Half tsp. dried thyme

Procedure:

1. Over high heat, heat 1/2 tablespoon olive oil in a large nonstick pan. Once the oil is sufficiently heated, add the pork chops and reduce the heat to medium-high.Cook chops for 3 minutes per side and adds the remaining 1/2 tablespoon of olive oil. Next, place them on a serving platter.
2. Add the apples and onion to the hot pan. Cook, turning often to prevent burning or sticking, for five min and when the veggies are cooked. In a small bowl, whisk together the stock and Dijon mustard while the apples and onion are boiling.
3. Stir in the sage and thyme to evenly coat the onion and apples in the pan. Return the pork chops to the pan with the stock mixture. Cook for 10-15 min, until the chop is done, covered in the pan. Allow 2 minutes for the pork chop to rest before carving.

Nutritional Value: Calories: 234, Fat: 11g, Carbs: 13g, Protein: 20g, Fiber: 3g, Sugar: 9g, Sodium: 290mg

25.3 Slow-Cooked Pineapple Pepper Pork

Prep Time: 10 mins. Cook Time: 5 hrs. Serves: 2 in 2 to 4 oz. portions

Ingredients:

- low-salt soy sauce or Bragg Liquid Aminos, 1/8 cup
- Juice of ¼ lemon

- Half tsp. garlic powder
- Half tsp. powdered cumin
- Quarter tsp. cayenne pepper
- one/eight tsp. powdered coriander
- ¾ pound boneless pork tenderloin
- 1 red capsicums, thinly sliced
- one (twenty-ounce) cans pineapple pieces in 100% natural juice or water, drained

Procedure:

1. In a shallow dish, combine the coriander, cayenne pepper, cumin, garlic powder, lemon juice, and soy sauce.
2. In a slow cooker, place the pork tenderloin and red capsicum pieces. Pia colada pieces and their juices on top Cover with the soy sauce mixture.
3. Cover the slow cooker with the cover and simmer on low for about 5 hrs. With a fork and tongs, shred the pork and continue to simmer on low for another twenty min, or until the juices have been soaked by the meat.

Nutritional Value: Calories: 131, Fat: 2g, Carbs: 11g, Protein: 17g, Fiber: 2g, Sugar: 8g, Sodium: 431mg

25.4 Pork and White Bean Soup

Prep Time: 10 mins. Cook Time: 40 mins. Serves: 3 cups in 1 cup portions

Ingredients:

- one tsp. Extra-virgn olive oil
- One average onion, cut
- 2 (4-ounce) boneless pork chops, one inch diced
- one (14.5 ounces) can tomatoes chopped
- 3 cups low-sodium chicken stock
- Half tsp. . dry thyme
- Quarter tsp. crushed pepper fakes(red)
- One (fifteen-ounce) can great northern beans, dry and rinsed
- eight ounces fresh spinach leaf

Procedure:

1. In a large soup pot or Dutch oven, heat the olive oil over medium heat.
2. Cook for 2 - 3 mins, or when the onion is soft. Cook for four to five mins after adding the meat.
3. Stir together the beans, red pepper flakes, thyme, tomatoes, and stock. Bring to a simmer, then turn down to low. Allow the soup to simmer, covered, for 30 minutes. 5 minutes after adding the spinach, stir it in until it has wilted. Serve immediately.

Nutritional Value: Calories: 156, Fat: 4g, Carbs: 17g, Protein: 17g, Fiber: 4g, Sugar: 6g, Sodium: 600mg

25.5 Traditional Pulled Pork

Prep Time: 5 mins. Cook Time: 6 hrs. Serves: 4

Ingredients:

- Half onion, peeled and cut into thick rings
- Half cup pork shoulder, trimmed
- ¼ tbsp. sodium chloride
- Quarter tsp. fresh powdered black-pepper
- Quarter tsp. garlic ground
- Quarter tsp. onion powder
- ¼ tbsp. paprika
- Half tbsp. Extra-virgn olive oil

Procedure:

1. Layer the onion pieces on the bottom of a 4- to 6-quart rice cooker, and then place the pork on top.
2. Mix the olive oil, paprika, onion powder, salt, garlic powder, and pepper in a shallow dish. Spread the mixture all over the meat to provide a uniform coating.
3. Cook on full flame for four to six hrs or on less heat for seven to eight hrs, or unless pork shreds easily. Discard the rendered fat and onions. Shred the pork

with two forks, and serve with your favorite sauce.

Nutritional Value: Calories: 562, Fat: 34g, Carbohydrates: 2g, Protein: 58g, Fiber: 1g, Sugar: 1g, Sodium: 1043mg

25.6 Hawaiian-Style Pork Skewers

Prep Time: 15 mins + 15 mins marinating, Cook Time: 20 mins. Serves: 2

Ingredients:

- one/eight cup low-salt soy-sauce
- Extra-virgn olive oil, one Half tbsps. divided
- 1 clove of garlic, minced
- Salts and fresh powdered black pepper
- 1/2 white onion, skinned and chopped into one-inched piece
- pineapple chunks, ¾ cups
- pork loin, diced into 1 Half-inch cubes, 1/2 pound
- Half red capsicum, trimmed, seeded, and diced into one-inched piece
- Half yellow-pepper, trimmed, seeded, and diced into one-inched piece

Procedure:

1. To avoid scorching, soak 4 to 5 wood skewers in water for 15 min. You may omit this step if you are using metal skewers.
2. Mix together the soy sauce, 3/4 tbsp olive oil, garlic, and sprinkle with salt to taste in a shallow dish. change side of the pork pieces in the salsa in the basin to evenly coat them. Allow for at least 15 min in the fridge.
3. Thread the pork, pineapple, onions, and peppers onto the skewers carefully, continuing until all of the ingredients are utilized. Brush the remaining tbsp of olive oil lightly on the meat and vegetables.

4. The grill is heated to high, then reduced to 400°F. Place the skewers on a grill. Sauté for three to four minutes on each side, then continue until the pork reaches an internal temperature of 145 degrees Fahrenheit. Serve without delay.

Nutritional Value: Calories: 292, Fat: 15g, Carbohydrates: 17g, Protein: 24g, Fiber: 2g, Sugar: 9g, Sodium: 979mg.

25.7 Honey-Mustard Glazed Pork Tenderloin with Haricot Verts

Prep Time: 10 mins. Cook Time: 30 mins + 15 mins rest. Serves: 2

Ingredients:

- Half tbsp. whole grain mustard
- Half tbsp. honey
- Half tbsp. soya sauce
- one small-sized clove of garlic, chopped
- ¼ tbsp. sriracha or mild hot sauce
- Sodium chloride
- Fresh powder black-pepper
- ¼ pound fresh beans green, cut
- Half tbsp Extra-virgn olive oil
- quarter pound trimmed pork tenderloin

Procedure:

1. In advance heat oven to 450°F. To catch the drippings, layer a baking skillet with foil of aluminum.
2. In a small dish, combine the mustard, honey, soy sauce, garlic, and sriracha. The salt should be added to taste. You may also add pepper
3. Spread the green beans on the baking sheet in a thin layer, and sprinkle with olive oil.
4. Place the meat on top of the green beans. Spread half of the sauce evenly over the meat.
5. Remove from oven after fifteen min, or until golden brown. Glaze the meat with the remaining sauce.Return the pork to

the oven for another 10 to 15 minutes, or until the internal temperature reaches 150 degrees Fahrenheit and the liquids are slightly transparent.

6. Take out of the oven and remove the pork with foil. Let rest for 11 to 14 min before slicing. Remove the pork from the oven and wrap it in aluminium foil. Wait 10 to 15 minutes before slicing.

Nutritional Value: Calories: 313, Fat: 9g, Carbohydrates: 26g, Protein: 36g, Fiber: 5g, Sugar: 17g, Sodium: 915mg

25.8 Pork Chipotle Tacos

Prep and Cook Time: 20 mins. Serves: 2 tacos

Ingredients:

- ¼ pound pork tenderloin
- Half tsp. chilies in adobo sauce (diced)
- Half tsp. garlic (chopped)
- quarter cup shallots (thin slices)
- Three fourth cup lemon juice, with its zest
- ¼ tbsp. lime juice
- Half tsp. oregano
- ¼ tsp. brown sugar
- ¼ tsp. salt
- Half tsps. olive oil
- Cooking spray
- Chopped cilantro
- 1 (6") corn tortilla
- 1/8 cup sour cream

Procedure:

1. Slice the pork into pieces to prepare it. In a dish with garlic, lime juice, chile, brown sugar, oregano, and salt, marinates the chicken.
2. Coat a nonstick pan with nonstick spray and heat it over moderate heat. Cook shallots for approximately four minutes, or until tender. Take the item out of the table.

3. Cook pork in a sauté pan until it is not pink anymore, about 3 minutes. Warm shallots in the pan with the shallots.
4. To assemble: heat up tortilla. On the tortilla arrange pork, sour cream, and cilantro.

Nutritional Value: Calories: 383 Fat: 18.9g Carb: 21.9g Protein: 33.1g, Fiber: 1.7g, Sugar: 8.3g, Sodium: 744mg

25.9 Sweet and Sour Pork

Prep Time: 15 mins. Cook Time: 30 mins. Serves: 6 cups in ½ cup portions

Ingredients:

- 1 tbsp. olive oil, divided
- Half lb. (450g) pork tenderloin, halved lengthwise and thinly sliced
- 1 tsp. Sodium chloride
- Half tsp. fresh powdered black pepper
- one little yellow onion, diced
- 1 capsicum , diced
- Half (12oz, 340g) bag frozen broccoli florets, thawed and patted dry
- Half (8oz, 227g) can water chestnuts, drained
- Half (8oz, 227g) can pineapple chunks, drained with Half cup juice reserved
- Rice vinegar, 1 tbsp.
- Soy sauce, 1 tbsp.
- Arrowroot powder, one tsp. (you can use cornstarch to substitute)
- Chopped fresh parsley, 1 tbsp. to garnish

Procedure:

1. In a non - stick pan, heat 1 tbsp oil over medium to high flame. Season the pork with a half tsp of salt and a quarter tsp. of pepper. Cook for another five min, or until the meat starts to golden. Place on a serving plate and set aside.
2. Remove any excess fat from the pan and warm the leftover 1 tbsp oil on medium to high heat. In a medium mixing dish,

combine the onion and peppers. Cook for 6 to 8 min, stirring periodically, after which the vegetables are slightly softened but still crisp. The skillet should have pork, broccoli, water chestnuts, and pineapple pieces. Cook for five min, swirling often.

3. Whisk together the reserved Half cup pineapple juice, vinegar, soy sauce, arrowroot, and the remaining Half tsp. salt and ¼ tsp. pepper. pour sauce to the skillet, and saute for 7 min, stir frequently unless well combined &

thickened. Serve hot, garnished with the chopped parsley.

Nutritional Value: Calories 137, Total Fat 4g, Total Carb 18g, Protein 10g, Fiber 3g, Sugar 13g, Sodium 589mg

26 SNACKS

26.1 Protein-Packed Pancakes

Prep Time: 5 mins. Cook Time: 5 mins. Serves: 2 pancakes

Ingredients:

- Egg-1
- low-fat cottage cheese- Half cup
- Whole wheat pastry flour two tbsp
- Melted coconut oil-1 ¼ tsp. s
- Nonstick cooking spray

Procedure:

1. Inside big dish, gently break the egg. Toss in few tbsps. of flour and coconut oil and whisk until they are all mixed together.
2. Spray a big pan or griddle with cooking oil and temp on average temp. Per pan cake, add one/three mug of batter to the pan. Each pancake should be cooked for 2 to 3 min, or till bubble develop on the top. Cook the second side of the pancakes for 1 to 2 minutes, or until golden.

Nutritional Value: Calories: 182, Fat: 10g, Carbs: 10g, Protein: 12g, Fiber: 3g, Sugar: 1g, Sodium: 68mg

26.2 Home-made Kefir

Prep Time: 5 mins. Cook Time: 12-48 hrs. Serves: 3 cups in ½ cup portions

Ingredients:

- 3 cups whole milk
- 1 tbsp. active kefir grains
- Fresh or frozen fruit (optional), to taste

Procedure:

1. Add the milk and kefir grains into a quart-size (1l) glass jar (do not use metal as this reacts with the grains), and stir to combine well. Wrap a paper towel or cheesecloth around the jar and attach it with a rubber band. Allow the jar to sit at 60–90°F (15–30°C) room temperature for as long as two days away from direct sunshine. Check the milk every few hours, the kefir is ready once it thickens to the consistency of a runny yogurt and tastes tangy. Once ready, pass it through a fine sieve and store. Add the kefir grains into a new batch of milk to make more.
2. Blend the fruit and kefir together in a blender until it is creamy. Refrigerate covered until ready to use. Kefir can be kept inside a fridge for as long as 14 days in an airtight container.

Nutritional Value: Calories: 74, Fat: 4g, Carb: 6g, Protein: 4g, Fiber: 0g, Sugar: 6g, Sodium: 53mg

26.3 Home-Made Yogurt

Prep Time: 10 mins. Cook Time: 15-18 h Serves: 4 cups in ½ cup portions

Ingredients:

- whole milk, 8 cups
- plain full-fat yogurt with live, active cultures- Half cup

Procedure:

1. Cover the milk in a slow cooker and simmer it on low for 2.5 hours until it reaches 185°F.
2. Turn off the slow cooker and let the milk sit for 3 hours or until it has cooled to 110–115°F (40–45°C).
3. Add the yogurt and let it sit for 10 hours covered, stirring occasionally. After three hours of refrigeration, serve the yogurt in an airtight container. Yogurt may be stored in the fridge for up to 14 days if it is kept in an airtight container.

Nutritional Value: Calories: 79, Fat: 4g, Carb: 6g, Protein: 4g, Fiber: 0g, Sugar: 7g, Sodium: 56mg

26.4 Sweet Potato Pancakes

Prep and Cook Time: 15 mins. Serves: 2

Ingredients:

- sweet potatoes, 1 lb.
- canola oil, 3 tbsps.
- garlic powder
- pepper, 1/2 tsp.
- whole-wheat flour, 3 tbsps. .
- organic eggs, 2

Procedure:

1. Steam the peeled sweet potatoes in a medium-heat steamer until they are just soft. Remove the sweet potatoes from the steamer once they have softened. Using a fork or potato masher, mash the ingredients until it's creamy and smooth.

2. In a large basin, thoroughly mash the sweet potatoes. Then, whisk in the flour and eggs completely. After adding the garlic powder and pepper, mix thoroughly. Place the sweet potato patties in an airtight container after shaping. Bring canola oil to a boil in a medium-sized saucepan. Cook sweet potato patties in a skillet over medium heat. The top should be starting to turn golden at this point. The sweet potato pancakes should be gently browned on both sides before re-cooking.

Nutritional Value: Calories: 1130, Fat: 51.8 g, Carbohydrates: 147.8g, Protein: 21g, Fiber: 19.8g, Sugar: 3.7g, Sodium: 166mg.

26.5 Mozzarella Sticks Amandine with Marinara Sauce*

Preparaton Time: 10 minutes plus 2 hours Freezing Time; Cooking Time: 6 minutes Serves: 6

Ingredients:

- Cornstarch, 1 tablespoon
- Almond Flour, 8 tablespoons
- Italian Seasoning, ½ teaspoon
- Salt, ¼ teaspoon
- Eggs, 2 large
- Mozzarella Sticks, 6 1-ounce pieces
- Extra-Virgin Olive Oil, 1 tablespoon

Procedure:

1. . Prepare your breading station. Place the cornstarch on a small plate. On a separate small plate, mix in the almond flour, Italian Seasoning and Salt. In a dish, thoroughly combine the eggs and lay them between the flour and cornstarch plates.
2. Halve the mozzarella sticks and coat each halved piece in the cornstarch, then the egg, then the almond flour mixture. Be sure that the mozzarella sticks are evenly coated to ensure that the

mozzarella does not leak out onto a baking sheet as it cooks. Repeat until all of the mozzarella pieces have been used up.

3. Cover and freeze the mozzarella sticks for two hours to ensure that they retain their structure. While this freezes, preheat an oven to 400 degrees Fahrenheit and line a cookie sheet with greaseproof paper.

4. After two hours, arrange the mozzarella sticks, evenly spaced an inch apart on the prepared cookie sheet. Lightly brush with the olive oil and bake for 4-6 minutes or until the cheese starts to bubble and the crust begins to turn golden. Watch carefully to ensure that the cheese does not completely melt. Serve warm.

Nutritional Value: Calories: 182, Fat: 15g, Carbohydrates: 4g, Protein: 11g, Fiber: 1g, Sugar: 1g, Sodium: 311mg.

26.6 Creamy Marinara Dipping Sauce*

Preparation Time: 5 minutes Cooking Time: 5 minutes Serves: ¾ cup

Ingredients:

- Non-fat, Plain Greek Yogurt, ½ cup
- Tomato Sauce, Low-Sodium, ½ cup
- Parmesan Cheese, 2 tablespoons, grated
- Italian Seasoning, 1 teaspoon
- Garlic Powder, ½ teaspoon
- Salt, ¼ teaspoon

Procedure:

1. Combine all of the ingredients in a saucepan and heat over a medium low flame.
2. Cook for 3-5 minutes. Be sure to stir frequently to prevent sticking at the bottom of the saucepan. The cheese should be completely melted and the sauce completely warmed through.

Nutritional Value: Calories: 36, Fat: 1g, Carbohydrates: 3g, Protein: 4g, Fiber: 2g, Sugar: 2g, Sodium: 226mg.

26.7 Cheesy Stuffed Mushroom Caps*

Preparation Time: 5 minutes Cooking Time: 20 minutes Serves: 12 caps

Ingredients:

- Button Mushroom Caps, 1 dozen
- Mozzarella Pearls, 4 ounces, fresh
- Almond Flour, 2 tablespoons
- Whipped Butter, 1 tablespoon
- Garlic Powder, ½ teaspoon
- Salt, 1/8 teaspoon

Procedure:

1. Preheat an oven to 350 degrees Fahrenheit and line a cookie sheet with Greaseproof Paper.
2. Brush the mushrooms and separate the cap from the stem. Arrange the mushrooms on the prepared cookie sheet, and top each with one piece of the mozzarella pearl.
3. Mix the remainder of the ingredients into a small bowl and sprinkle over the prepared mushroom caps. Bake in an oven that has been prepared until the cheese has melted. Serve hot.

Nutritional Value: Calories: 117, Fat: 9g, Carbohydrates: 4g, Protein: 8g, Fiber: 1g, Sugar: 0.25g, Sodium: 141mg.

26.8 Cheesy Cauliflower Bites*

Preparation Time: 5 minutes Cooking Time: 15 minutes Serves: 4

Ingredients:

- Mozzarella Cheese, ½ cup, shredded
- Cauliflower Rice, 1 cup
- Almond Flour, ½ cup
- Egg, 1 large

- Cornstarch, 1 tablespoon
- Salt, ¼ teaspoon

Procedure:

1. Preheat the oven to 400 degrees Fahrenheit., Line a large cookie sheet with greaseproof paper and set aside.
2. Combine all of the ingredients in a large bowl and mix until well incorporated. Scoop the mixture into heaping tablespoons and arrange on the prepared baking sheet, evenly spaced. This should make about 16 pieces.
3. Bake for 13 to 15 minutes or until golden brown and crisp. Serve warm with the Creamy Marinara Sauce.

Nutritional Value: Calories: 152, Fat: 11g, Carbohydrates: 6g, Protein: 9g, Fiber: 2g, Sugar: 1g, Sodium: 253mg.

26.9 Herbed Muffins Italienne*

Preparation Time: 5 minutes Cooking Time: 15 minutes. Serves: 4

Ingredients:

- Non-stick Cooking Spray, 1 sec
- Almond Flour, 8 tablespoons
- Parmesan Cheese, ¼ cup, shredded
- Egg, 1 large
- Garlic Powder, 1 teaspoon
- Italian Seasoning, 1 teaspoon
- Baking Powder, 1 teaspoon
- Salt, ¼ teaspoon

Procedure:

1. Preheat an oven to 350 degrees Fahrenheit and line a muffin pan with 4 paper liners. Spray the prepared liners with the cooking spray and set aside.
2. Combine the remainder of the ingredients in a large bowl until well incorporated. Use a scoop and scoop the batter into the prepared and lined muffin trays and bake for 12 minutes or unti golden brown on top, and a skewer

inserted into the center of the muffin comes out clean. Serve warm.

Nutritional Value: Calories: 128, Fat: 10g, Carbohydrates: 5g, Protein: 7g, Fiber: 2g, Sugar: 1g, Sodium: 217mg.

26.10 Cheese Biscuits*

Preparation Time: 5 minutes Cooking Time: 15 minutes Serves: 8

Ingredients:

- Almond Flour, 1 cup
- Parmesan Cheese, ¼ cup, shredded
- Cheddar Cheese, ¼ cup, shredded
- Baking Powder, 2 teaspoons
- Garlic Powder, 2 teaspoons
- Salt, ½ teaspoon
- Eggs, 2 large, whole

Procedure:

1. Preheat an oven to 350 degrees Fahrenheit. Prepare a baking sheet with nonstick paper and set aside.
2. Combine all of the dry ingredients in a large bowl until well incorporated. Crack the eggs individually and whisk them into the biscuit batter.
3. Place a heaping dollop of the mixture on the prepared baking sheet using a tablespoon.With a spatula, flatten the dough into 2-inch circles. Make sure that these are evenly spaced. This should form about 8 biscuits. Bake for 15 minutes or until golden brown. Serve warm.

Nutritional Value: Calories: 275, Fat: 23g, Carbohydrates: 8g, Protein: 15g, Fiber: 3g, Sugar: 1g, Sodium: 447mg.

26.11 Sesame Sugar Snap Pea Chips

Prep Time: 5 mins. Cook Time: 20 mins. Serves: 2

Ingredients:

- Half lb. (450g) sugar snap peas, trimmed
- Half tsp. sesame oil
- 1 tbsp. sesame seeds
- Half tsp. sodium chloride
- quarter tsp. fresh black pepper powder

Procedure:

1. Preheat the oven to 450 degrees Fahrenheit. Line a baking sheet with parchment paper. In a large mixing bowl, combine all ingredients and toss in the peas to coat evenly.
2. Transfer the coated peas to the prepared baking sheet and layer thoroughly into one layer. Bake for 20 minutes or until crispy. Let cool completely before eating and store in an air tight container for later consumption.

Nutritional Value: Calories 111, Total Fat 5g, Total Carb 13g, Protein 5g, Fiber 5g, Sugar 6g, Sodium 7mg

26.12 Spiced Peanuts

Prep Time: 10 mins. Cook Time: 20 mins. Serves: 5, 3 oz. per portion

Ingredients:

- Half lb. (450g) unsalted roasted peanuts
- Half tsp. olive oil
- Half tsp. ground chili
- Quarter tsp. cumin powder
- Half tsp. paprika(smoked)
- Ground garlic quarter tsp.
- Ground onion quarter tsp.
- Dry oregano half tsp. .
- Salt Half tsp.
- Fresh black pepper powder quarter tsp.

Procedure:

1. Preheat ovens to 300 degrees Fahrenheit (180 degrees Celsius) (150 degrees Celsius). Lining a baking sheet with a rubber mat or wax paper.
2. Combine all ingredients in a large bowl until they are uniformly covered. The

peanuts should be spread out on a baking sheet for 10 minutes. Remove the baking sheet from the oven and shake it to get the peanuts to spread evenly around the baking sheet. After returning the baking sheet to the range, bake for an additional 9 minutes. Allow cooling completely before placing it in an airtight container.

Nutritional Value : Calories 547, Total Fat 46g, Total Carb 21g, Protein 22g, Fiber 8g, Sugar 5g, Sodium 487mg

26.13 Maple-Roasted Brussels Sprout

Prep Time: 15 mins. Cook Time: 30 mins. Serves: 2 cups

Ingredients:

- Half lb. (450g) Brussels sprouts, cut and half
- one small carrot, divided into Half-in (1.25cm) slices
- Half tbsp olive-oil
- Half tsp. Sodium chloride
- ¼ tsp. fresh black pepper powder
- one tbsp whole-grain mustard
- Half tbsp. pure maple syrup
- ¼ cup pecans, roughly chopped

Procedure:

1. turn the microwave to 400 °F (200 degrees Celsius) and prepare a cookie sheet or a rubber mat.
2. In a large mixing bowl, toss the Brussels sprouts, carrots, olive oil, salt, and pepper until equally coated. Put veggies on the cookie sheet in a thin layer and roast for thirty min, or until the veggies are caramelised around the margins.
3. Whisk together the mustard and maple syrup in a basin and leave aside while the vegetables roast. Take the roasted veggies from oven and immediately shift them to dish having mustard-maple glaze. Add the pecans, and mix until all the ingredients are coated.

Nutritional Value: Calories 144, Total Fat 9g, Total Carb 14g, Protein 4g, Fiber 5g, Sugar 6g, Sodium 562mg

26.14 Turkey Bacon Dijon Brussels Sprouts

Prep Time: 10 mins. Cook Time: 20 mins. Serves: 2 cups in ½ cup portions

Ingredients:

- 1 strip turkey bacon
- Half tbsp. olive oil
- 1 small minced white onion
- Half lb. (450g) Brussels sprouts, trimmed and halved
- ¼ cup beef stock
- 1 tbsp. Dijon mustard
- Half tbsp. white vinegar
- Half tsp. sodium chloride
- Quarter tsp. Fresh black pepper powder

Procedure:

1. Heat a big nonstick skillet on average temp. saute your bacon for 4 minutes on each side or until crisp. Shift your bacon to a plate layered using paper sheets to absorb any rendered grease. Remove the bacon grease.
2. After increasing the temperature to medium-high, olive oil is added. When the pan is hot, equally distribute the onion and Brussels sprouts. If the vegetables begin to caramelize, continue to sauté for another five minutes. They should not be disturbed. While the veggies are cooking, combine the vinegar, mustard, salt, and pepper in a small bowl and whisk until smooth.
3. A cup of chicken stock should accompany cooked veggies after they have begun to caramelize. Add a cover and lower the temperature to a more moderate setting. Cover the pan with a cover and cook for four minutes. The liquid should have thickened enough to glaze the sprouts after another five minutes of sautéing, stirring periodically.

4. Add chopped pieces to the pan. Mix well and serve.

Nutritional Value: Calories 122, Total Fat 5g, Total Carb 14g, Protein 6g, Fiber 5g, Sugar 4g, Sodium 947mg

26.15 Asparagus Amandine

Prep Time: 5 mins. Cook Time: 10 mins Serves: 2 cups in ½ cup portions

Ingredients:

- Half cup slivered almonds
- Half lb. (450g) medium-thick asparagus
- Half tbsp. olive oil
- Half cup diced shallot
- 1 tsp. salt, divided
- One garlic clove, chopped
- Half tbsp. butter
- ¼tsp. Fresh black pepper powder
- Half tsp. freshly squeezed lemon juice
- Crumbled feta cheese (optional)

Procedure:

1. Prepare a large skillet over medium temperature. Stir in the bread and almonds for 2 - 3 mins, till gently toasted but not burned. Place the mixture in a small basin and put it aside. Trim the bottom third of the asparagus and discard it. Trim the asparagus stalks and cut them into 2-in (5-cm) segments.
2. In a big skillet, warm the olive oil over moderate to high temperature. When the pan is heated, adding the shallot, 1 tsp. salt, and asparagus, and cook until everything is thoroughly mixed. Cook, stirring periodically, for 5 to 7 min.
3. Make an open area: Reduce the temperature to medium and push the shallot and asparagus towards the skillet edges. In the middle of the pan, drop the garlic and cook for thirty seconds, or until aromatic. Season with salt and pepper after adding the butter. Mix until everything is completely blended. Remove the turn off the heat and drizzle with lemon juice before

scattering the roasted almonds on top. Toss until everything is evenly distributed.

Nutritional Value: Calories 107, Total Fat 8g, Total Carb 7g, Protein 4g, Fiber 3g, Sugar 3g, Sodium 779mg

26.16 Roasted Beets with Summer Greens

Prep Time: 15 mins. Cook Time: 30 mins Serves: 4 oz. per serving

Ingredients:

For the dressing:

- Half tsp. nicely grated lemon zest
- one/eight cup freshly squeezed lime
- Half tbsp. plain Greek yogurt
- one small shallot, finely grated
- ¼ tsp. salt
- ¼ tsp. Fresh black pepper powdered

For the salad:

- two golden beets, sliced (regular beets are fine, too)
- Half tsp. olive-oil
- Half tsp. sodium chloride
- Quarter tsp. fresh black pepper powder
- one Half tbsp. pine nuts
- Halflb (450g) asparagus
- 2 oz.(170g) arugula

Procedure:

1. Prepare the oven to 400 ° F. (200 degrees Celsius). Using parafilm or a baking mat, line a baking sheet.
2. Place the beets in a single layer on the baking sheet and drizzle with pepper, salt, and olive oil. Toss to coat. Roast for 25 minutes or until fork-tender on a baking sheet in a single layer. Allow time for the liquid to cool completely. While you're waiting, whip up a batch of the dressing. All ingredients should be combined in a small dish and set aside.
3. In a small saucepan over heat that is average to weak, toast the pine nuts, frequently stirring, for 4 to 5 min, or until golden-ish brown. Allow cooling. Trim and discard the asparagus stems' bottom third. Carefully slice the asparagus lengthwise into paper-thin strips using a vegetable peeler or mandolin. (Make use of the guard.)
4. In a big serving bowl, place the asparagus strips, beets, (arugula), pine nuts, & dressing and mix well before serving.

Nutritional Value: Calories 167, Total Fat 10g, Total Carb 17g, Protein 6g, Fiber 6g, Sugar 8g, Sodium 942mg

26.17 Balsamic-Glazed Haricot-Verts

Prep Time: 10 mins. Cook Time: 15 mins. Serves: 2 cups in ½ cup portions

Ingredients:

- Half tsp. coconut oil, melted, or olive oil
- Half cup diced shallots
- Half cup (450g) green-beans, cut and chopped
- One little clove garlic, minced
- Half cup halved cherry tomatoes
- 1 tbsp. balsamic vinegar
- Half tbsp. butter
- Half tsp. sodium chloride
- Quarter tsp. fresh black pepper powder

Procedure:

1. For 2 minutes, preheat a large nonstick skillet over high heat. The shallots and green beans are cooked in a pan with coconut oil. Stir often for four minutes, or until the green beans are blistering and the shallots are caramelising. To the pan, add the garlic and tomatoes. Combine well. Reduce to a moderate temp. saute for five min covered.
2. take the cover off, and pour the vinegar & butter to the skillet. saute for five min, stir occasionally, till the liquid has been thickened enough to glaze the vegetables. Season with sodium chloride

& pepper to taste, and mix till well coated.

Nutritional Value: Calories 76, Total Fat 3g, Total Carb 12g, Protein 2g, Fiber 3g, Sugar 6g, Sodium 11mg

26.18 Sausage Cornbread

Prep and Cook Time: 30 mins. Serves: 4 slices

Ingredients:

- one package (8.5 oz.) corn muffin mixture
- one package (8 oz.) meatless Breakfast Links, chopped or other sausage
- 2% milk, 1 cup
- minced onion, 1/2 cup
- minced celery, 1/2 cup
- ¼ cup no-cholesterol egg product, or one egg

Procedure:

1. Blend every the content. place in a loaf pan or nine inched pie dish sprayed with nonstick spray. oven at four twenty five degrees F for twenty five minutes or until golden-ish brown.

Nutritional Value: Calories: 744, Fat: 26.7g, Carbs: 68.3g, Protein: 57.5g, Fiber: 11g, Sugar: 30.5g, Sodium: 2049mg

26.19 Spiced Cornbread

Prep and Cook Time: 45 mins. Serves 4

Ingredients:

- half cup plus one tsp. Wheat Cereal Cream uncooked
- one cup flour
- One tsp. Ground Chili
- one tbsp. Calumet Baking Powder
- quarter cup of no-cholesterol egg product
- half cup no-fat milk
- 1 tbsp. in liquid state Margarine or butter
- three tbsps. Honey
- one cup corn, mashed
- Half cup ripped low-Fat Sharp (Cheddar)Cheese

Procedure:

1. Take a 9-inch baking dish or loaf pan and put a tablespoon of oil in the bottom.
2. Dissolve yeast and chili into a large bowl of leftover cereal. Stir to combine. Gather all wet ingredients in a large bowl: milk, egg substitute, and margarine. Add the dry ingredients one at a time, whisking until the mixture is just moistened. Stir in the cheese and corn until well blended, then place in the pan that has already been preheated. Heat the oven to 340°F and bake for 30 minutes or until lightly browned, stirring halfway through baking.

Nutritional Value: Calories: 1074, Fat: 22.5g, Carbs: 192.4g, Protein: 42.6g, Fiber: 19.4g, Sugar: 63.3g, Sodium: 1217mg.

27 9-WEEK MEAL PLAN FOR THE GASTRIC BYPASS DIET

I prepared a meal plan for 9 weeks which is about 2 months. Repeating this meal plan 6 times throughout the year, starting from the first week after the tenth, you will have concluded your annual nutrition plan. To ensure the habit of this diet and the results, we recommend applying it for 3 years, consequently for a total of 1000 days. The meal plans here are not meant to be a strict interpretation of what you would have to eat after surgery, as this is entirely dependent on economics, as well as the nutritional requirements that your doctor would prescribe. As it stands in these charts, the meal plans here are designed for a person who has fully recovered from the surgery and is able to resume intake of solid foods. Some recipes may yield more than one portion of the dish, so you can repurpose any leftovers to last you throughout the week. Breakfast and snacks especially have recipes that yield numerous servings, which you can spread throughout the week. A lot of the recipes involve advanced preparation, and this would be handy, especially if you need quick breakfasts on the go. A note that must be taken into consideration here involves the snacks and appetizers as the integration of these dishes are purely in between mealtimes, and are dependent on your personal preference. Most of these recipes are filling in themselves, but can be paired with any of the side dishes listed under Chapter 9 and in Chapter 4 for the produce. Mix and match the recipes according to what is in your pantry, and what your budget calls for.

27.1 Week 1 (Clear Liquid Diet)

	Breakfast	AM Snack	Lunch	PM Snack	Supper
Day 1	Bone Stock		Cannellini and Bone Broth		Protein Packed Milk
Day 2	Chicken Broth		Leftover Bone Stock		Fresh Strawberry Smoothie
Day 3	Clear Vegetable Broth		Basic Beef Bone Broth		Citrus Mousse
Day 4	Leftover Cannellini and Bone Broth	Water or Calorie Free Drink	Leftover Bone Stock	Water or Calorie Free Drink	Tropical Popsicles
Day 5	Leftover Basic Beef Bone Broth		Leftover Clear Vegetable Broth		Watermelon and Basil Granita
Day 6	Leftover Bone Stock		Leftover Basic Beef Bone Broth		Protein Packed Milk
Day 7	Leftover Chicken Broth		Leftover Cannellini and Bone Broth		Tropical Popsicles

27.2 Week 2 (Pureed Diet)

	Breakfast	AM Snack	Lunch	PM Snack	Supper
Day 1	Split Pea Soup		High-Protein Fruit Smoothie		Cauliflower Mash
Day 2	Creamed Broccoli Chowder		Spring Clean Green Protein Shake		Oriental Hummus
Day 3	Cream of Cauliflower Soup		Superpacked Shake		Baba Ganoush
Day 4	Spring Pea Soup	Water or Calorie Free Drink	Leftover Split Pea Soup	Water or Calorie Free Drink	Leftover Creamed Broccoli Chowder
Day 5	Roasted Carrot and Ginger Soup		Superpacked Shake		Cauliflower Mash
Day 6	Leftover Split Pea Soup		Leftover Roasted Carrot and Ginger Soup		Dreamsicle Smoothie
Day 7	Leftover Cream of Cauliflower Soup		Chinese Egg Roll Bowl		Chocolate Protein Shake

27.3 Week 3 (Pureed Diet)

	Breakfast	AM Snack	Lunch	PM Snack	Supper
Day 1	Scrambled Egg Burritos		Spring Vegetable and Chicken Puree		Superpacked Shake
Day 2	Scrambled Egg with Aged Cheddar		Pizza Puree		Puree of Butternut
Day 3	Scrambled Egg Burritos		Citrus Sunrise Shake		Spring Pea Soup
Day 4	Scrambled Egg with Aged Cheddar	Water or Calorie Free Drink	Puree of Butternut	Water or Calorie Free Drink	Very Berry Protein Shake
Day 5	Cheese Pommes Puree		Spring Clean Green Protein Shake		Spring Vegetable and Chicken Puree
Day 6	Scrambled Egg Burritos		Cauliflower Mash		Oriental Hummus
Day 7	Pizza Puree		Pizza Puree		Leftover Spring Pea Soup

27.4 Week 4 (Soft Food Phase)

	Breakfast	AM Snack	Lunch	PM Snack	Supper
Day 1	Citrus Sunrise Shake	Water or Calorie Free Drink	Guiltless Corn-Crusted Cod	Water or Calorie Free Drink	Chili con Pavo
Day 2	Chocolate Protein Smoothie		Leftover Chili con Pavo		Leftover Guiltless Corn-Crusted Cod
Day 3	Very Berry Protein Shake		Home-style Turkey Meatloaf		Sweet and Tart Baked Halibut
Day 4	Root Beer Float Protein Shake		Pesto-Glazed Salmon		Leftover Turkey Meatloaf
Day 5	Citrus Sunrise Shake		Leftover Baked Halibut		Leftover Chili con Pavo
Day 6	Superpacked Shake		Asian-Chicken Lettuce Wraps		West Coast Seafood Stew
Day 7	Banana Split protein Shake		Leftover West Coast Seafood Stew		Leftover Chicken Wraps

27.5 Week 5 (Soft Food Phase)

	Breakfast	AM Snack	Lunch	PM Snack	Supper
Day 1	Scrambled Egg Burritos	Water or Calorie Free Drink	Chili con Pollo	Water or Calorie Free Drink	Summery Lemon Crab Cakes
Day 2	Chocolate Chia Pudding		Leftover Crab Cakes		Leftover Chili con Pollo
Day 3	Scrambled Egg Burritos		Mexican Style Red Snapper		Creamy Chicken Cauliflower Soup
Day 4	Chocolate Chia Pudding		Leftover Cauliflower Soup		Leftover Snapper
Day 5	Scrambled Egg Burritos		Barley with Chicken Vegetable Soup		Shrimp Cocktail Greens
Day 6	Chocolate Chia Pudding		Not Your Mom's Tuna Noodle Casserole		Leftover Barley Soup
Day 7	Scrambled Egg Burritos		Leftover Casserole		Leftover Cocktail Greens

27.6 Week 6 (Stabilization Phase)

	Breakfast	AM Snack	Lunch	PM Snack	Supper
Day 1	Avocado Toast with Hard-Boiled Eggs		Buffalo Chicken Tortilla Wraps		Chinese Egg Roll Bowl
Day 2	Chicken Pasta Salad		Leftover Egg Roll Bowl		Leftover Tortilla Wraps
Day 3	Avocado Toast with Hard-Boiled Eggs		Fried Rice		Vegetarian Lasagna Roll-ups
Day 4	Fall Chicken Salad	Water or Calorie Free Drink	Leftover Rollups	Water or Calorie Free Drink	Leftover Fried Rice
Day 5	Avocado Toast with Hard-Boiled Eggs		Chicken Cordon Bleu		Turkey Bacon Potato Soup
Day 6	Fall Chicken Salad		Leftover Potato Soup		Chopped Greek Salad
Day 7	Avocado Toast with Hard-Boiled Eggs		Leftover Cordon Bleu		Waldorf-Chicken Salad

27.7 Week 7 (Stabilization Phase)

	Breakfast	AM Snack	Lunch	PM Snack	Supper
Day 1	Chicken Pasta Salad		West Coast Seafood Stew		Slow-Cooked Beef Sandwiches
Day 2	Turkey Tostadas		Leftover Beef Sandwiches		Leftover Seafood Stew
Day 3	Chicken Pasta Salad		Cauliflower Couscous		Vegetarian Chow Mein
Day 4	Turkey Tostadas	Water or Calorie Free Drink	Traditional Pulled Pork	Water or Calorie Free Drink	Turkey Rollatini
Day 5	Chicken Pasta Salad		Chicken Jambalaya		Leftover Chow Mein
Day 6	Turkey Tostadas		Leftover Jambalaya		Leftover Pulled Pork
Day 7	Chicken Pasta Salad		Leftover Rollatini		Leftover Couscous

27.8 Week 8 (Stabilization Phase)

	Breakfast	AM Snack	Lunch	PM Snack	Supper
Day 1	Baked Mozzarella and Onion Egg Muffins	Water or Calorie Free Drink	Hawaiian Style Pork-Skewers	Water or Calorie Free Drink	Pork Chipotle Tacos
Day 2	Protein Packed Pancakes		Home-made Turkey Sausage		Basic Poached Chicken
Day 3	Baked Mozzarella and Onion Egg Muffins		Leftover Pork Skewers		Leftover Poached Chicken
Day 4	Protein Packed Pancakes		Leftover Turkey Sausage		Leftover Tacos
Day 5	Baked Mozzarella and Onion Egg Muffins		Spiced Pulled Pork		Roasted Vegetables
Day 6	Protein Packed Pancakes		Colonial Vegetable Beef Stew		Leftover Pulled Pork
Day 7	Baked Mozzarella and Onion Egg Muffins		Leftover Beef Stew		Leftover Vegetables

27.9 Week 9 (Stabilization Phase)

	Breakfast	AM Snack	Lunch	PM Snack	Supper
Day 1	Scrambled Egg Burritos	Water or Calorie Free Drink	Chicken Tikka Masala	Water or Calorie Free Drink	Surf and Turf Gumbo
Day 2	Sweet Potato Pancakes		Leftover Gumbo		Leftover Chicken Tikka Masala
Day 3	Scrambled Egg Burritos		Turkey Meatballs with Vegetable Spaghetti		Turkey Meatballs with Vegetable Spaghetti
Day 4	Mini Vegetarian Pizzas		Chicken Bell-Pepper Vegetable Nachos		Leftover Nachos
Day 5	Scrambled Egg Burritos		Country Style Chicken Tenders		One-Pan Autumn Pork Chops
Day 6	Mini Vegetarian Pizzas		Leftover Pork Chops		Turkey Salad
Day 7	Scrambled Egg Burritos		Leftover Turkey Salad		Leftover Chicken Tenders

Printed in Great Britain
by Amazon